PRAISE FOR *CHANGE STARTS WITH YOU*

"We are all better people because we get the opportunity to know and, most importantly, learn from my dear friend Sam Acho. He is motivation and inspiration personified. In a world full of news, hot takes, and clickbait built to tear us apart, Sam's insight and perspective bring us together. He shows us how finding our inner power and purpose can ignite progress, because change truly starts with us."

— CHINEY OGWUMIKE, WNBA ALL-STAR AND ESPN BROADCASTER

"I first connected with Sam on the West Side of Chicago on a trip to learn more about . . . the community. I was humbled and honored to be a member of the group that took the initiative to be a part of the solution. With Sam and his family being from Nigeria, the other athletes and I quickly saw that there was no better leader to bring us together and make a difference. This is why I genuinely believe there is not a better person to share a story like this with the world. Life is the process of what we learn every day and the way we handle whatever comes our way. What started off as a spark of hope turned into a fire of transformation. I saw a city changed, one person at a time. You can be a part of that same change. You can be a part of even bigger change. You can change the world. The lessons in this book helped show me that truth. My hope is that it shows you the same."

— JASON HEYWARD, MLB ALL-STAR, WORLD SERIES
CHAMPION, AND 5-TIME GOLD GLOVE WINNER

"Now more than ever we need dreamers, but unfortunately we are living in an era when culture is quick to cancel people instead of cultivate them. As a result many conform to the ways of this world, and their dreams are often delayed or detoured. Sam Acho's insightful words and his inspirational stories found within the pages of this book will not only ignite your God-given dream into a fiery reality but also empower you with the faith needed to keep that dream from being extinguished by fear."

— JASON WILSON, BESTSELLING AUTHOR AND FOUNDER OF THE
CAVE OF ADULLAM TRANSFORMATIONAL TRAINING ACADEMY

"A heart for change is incomplete without a willingness to walk. For as long as I have known him, Sam has exhibited both, courageously inspiring others to step outside of fears and boundaries to enter into culture-shifting purpose. *Change Starts With You* is an overflow of a life God has blessed to be a blessing to others. Prepare to be ignited!"

— BENJAMIN WATSON, AUTHOR, BROADCASTER, AND VICE
    PRESIDENT OF STRATEGIC RELATIONSHIPS FOR HUMAN COALITION

"*Change Starts With You* helps you to embrace the idea that to be a change agent for good, you needn't be a finished work yourself. The stories and practical advice contained within the pages can free the reader to act in pursuit of what is beckoning their humanity. Sparks of thoughtfulness will meet embers that fuel the way to greater good through consistency and community. I found myself encouraged, because often I am riddled with doubt, convinced I am terribly audacious to believe myself capable of shifting things. But within these chapters are true, substantive, and incremental changes, evidenced by people who pushed past their unbelief. Thank you, Sam, and bless you. I look forward to the way the information contained here is digested and to the many blossoms that will come from your need to contribute and be of service."

— ESSENCE ATKINS, ACTRESS AND HUMANITARIAN

"Sam is a refreshing voice that the world so needs right now. He provides the encouragement (or confidence) that we've always had the power within to accomplish our dreams and build others to do the same. We don't need to wait for anyone else to make it happen; change starts with us. This book is not a 'how to,' but a 'to do.' Sam is the spark to refire and refuel you like only Sam can, to become a force for good and live the unlimited life we've imagined in both a relatable and aspirational way. He is one of the most courageous and thoughtful people I know, whom I respect and admire deeply. I am proud to call him a friend and colleague. I can't wait for him to inspire you to take action in the same way he's inspired me. Thank you for being you, Sam. Let's go!"

— MOLLY QERIM, HOST OF *FIRST TAKE* ON ESPN AND PHILANTHROPIST

CHANGE
STARTS
WITH
YOU

CHANGE
STARTS
WITH
YOU

**FOLLOWING
YOUR FIRE
TO HEAL A
BROKEN WORLD**

SAM ACHO

NELSON
BOOKS

An Imprint of Thomas Nelson

Change Starts with You

Published in Nashville, Tennessee, by Nelson Books, an imprint of Thomas Nelson. Nelson Books and Thomas Nelson are registered trademarks of HarperCollins Christian Publishing, Inc.

Published in association with The Bindery Agency, www.TheBinderyAgency.com.

Thomas Nelson titles may be purchased in bulk for educational, business, fund-raising, or sales promotional use. For information, please email SpecialMarkets@ThomasNelson.com.

ISBN 978-1-4002-3795-1 (eBook)
ISBN 978-1-4002-3799-9 (HC)

Library of Congress Cataloging-in-Publication Data on File

Printed in the United States of America

22 23 24 25 26 LBC 5 4 3 2 1

This book is dedicated to
my Helper, Comforter, and Friend.
God has been so kind to me.
Excited for what we get to build together.

CONTENTS

FOREWORD

by Gary Haugen

At the time Sam Acho's book first came to me, the world had already been experiencing the most accelerated era of change in human history. Then a global pandemic, economic volatility, a war in Europe, and deep political and ideological divisions intensified the sense of chaos and confusion.

Indeed, I believe these moments of difficulty and disorientation expose our deep yearnings for meaning, significance, and clarity of purpose. It's for this reason that I'm so grateful for the authentic and vulnerable wisdom articulated throughout Sam's book. From cover to cover, his words offer us a refreshing perspective on what it looks like to find joy in fulfilling our purpose—even in our darkest moments.

For most of my life, I've wrestled with how to

find my purpose in a broken world. Before I founded International Justice Mission (IJM) in 1997, I was the United Nation's lead investigator on the Rwandan genocide, and I witnessed some of the darkest sides of humanity. In such moments the suffering and evil in the world can feel overwhelming. How could any of us make a difference with our lives? But as Sam reminds us in the pages to come, these places of hopelessness and despair are where our light can shine the brightest—not in spite of the darkness but because of it. Put simply, the people of God are most who they are meant to be when the world is least as it was meant to be.

Jesus explains this to his followers in Matthew 5 when he says that we are to be the light and salt of the earth. Just as light finds its power and purpose in darkness and salt finds its power and purpose in decay, we are also invited to discover and live out our redemptive purpose in a fallen world.

Sam provides inspiring and practical guidance on how we can personally apply this teaching. His steady virtue through the ups and downs of life offers a shining example of what it means to live out our purpose with joy.

He had joined us at IJM headquarters as part of the NFLPA externship program and provided insights and critical research that helped us launch a brand-new field office in Romania. Not long after that, he led a trip to our field office in Guatemala, where he spent meaningful time with children who had recently been rescued from horrific exploitation and abuse. He came alongside our frontline colleagues, who come face-to-face with unimaginable violence every day. He poured into them, encouraged them, and prayed with them for strength to accomplish the heavy work set before them. Sam decided to say yes to stepping into the ugly reality of child abuse in order to bring rescue and restoration, because that's who Sam is.

But what Sam humbly shows throughout his book is that this life-changing, supernatural love that brings light into the darkest places isn't reserved for NFL stars, influencers, or super-spiritual Christians who have everything figured out. Rather, it's something Jesus enables all of us to take part in as he calls us to bring his light and draw close to the pain and suffering in the world.

What I've seen in Sam is not an isolated example of supernatural love. I've seen it lived out through hundreds—if not thousands—of similar stories where ordinary, imperfect, and broken people decided to heed Jesus' call to be salt and light and find their transformative power and purpose in the darkness and decay of the world.

As Sam leads by example, he poignantly reminds us that at any moment we could be someone's answered prayer. All that's needed is that we find the courage to say yes to small steps of faith and show up authentically just as we are—in all our vulnerability, brokenness, and imperfection—so that we might bring healing to a broken world.

I have no doubt that, as you make your way through this book, you will feel renewed, invigorated, and inspired to courageously say yes to whatever work of love Jesus is calling you into next. May you be as encouraged as I was to be pointed towards the deep joy of fulfilling your purpose as a light that shines brightly in the darkness.

Gary Haugen
Founder and CEO of
International Justice Mission

INTRODUCTION

Heat is a powerful force with some amazing qualities. It brings out the best *and* the worst in things.
Let me explain.

When gold or silver is put into a crucible over a
fire, the impurities (known as "dross") rise to the top.
When faced with extreme heat, these precious met-
als are purified. Cleansed. Nothing about the metal's
essential makeup changes, but the impurities in them
are brought to the surface. These impurities are then
removed, leaving behind pure silver, precious gold.

America is in a crucible right now. You might be too.

Not long ago, all of America witnessed homicide
firsthand, and we don't know what to do with that
experience. Many African Americans have been crying
out for help for years, to no avail. But after the murder
of George Floyd, the unarmed Black man in Minnesota
who was choked to death by a police officer while three

other officers stood idly by, America was unavoidably confronted with the disturbing reality that racial injustice is not a thing of the past.

There was no escape. We couldn't get away from the heat. And we are still living in that country-defining moment. The impurity of racism, an evil that has existed in the fiber of American history ever since slaves were first brought over in 1619, has now risen to the top. And now that we see it, it's time to remove it.

This book, at its core, is about taking things that are broken—systems, situations, people—and working toward making them whole. Sometimes that brokenness is on the outside. Cities, countries, and the communities in which we live, work, and play. Other times that brokenness is within. And until we address the things that break our hearts, the things that bring us pain, we won't be able to do what we were put on this earth to do.

What breaks your heart? What brings you joy? When do you feel shame? Everything you want is on the other side of these questions.

I have a friend who's working on changing the world. But he needed a little help. And then he got it, or so he thought. He had a conversation with someone who possessed the exact thing he needed to make the change he wanted to see. They were on board to help, but they backed out at the last minute. Their text message read, Thanks so much, but after further consideration, I will be unable to participate. I'm praying for you.

My friend was frustrated. *Don't say you're just praying for me when you're literally the answer to my prayers!*

You are the answer to someone's prayers. Your actions, your ears, your words, your feet, your belief. Show up. I heard a saying from a coach: "You follow with your feet." If you're a leader and you claim people are following you, see how many feet are behind you. If there aren't that many, you may need to reevaluate your leadership style. On the other hand, if you're following someone with your words but not with your actions, I would question what kind of love that is. Suffice it to say, don't tell someone that you're praying for them when you are the answer to their prayers. Just go.

One of my favorite passages in the Bible is about love. It's likely one you've heard before. "Love is patient, love is kind. It does not envy, it does not boast, it is not proud. It does not dishonor others, it is not self-seeking, it is not easily angered, it keeps no record of wrongs. Love does not delight in evil but rejoices with the truth. It always protects, always trusts, always hopes, always perseveres. Love never fails."[1] So if you love me, if you love anyone, act like it.

I'll let you in on a little secret. People in the writing world often talk about a *through line*, the main message of a book. My through line is this: I want you to know about the joy of heaven on earth. The joy of seeking justice and journeying toward a better tomorrow. But the workers are few, and change starts with you.

I want to empower, encourage, and equip you with a simple but controversial truth: you *can* make a difference; you *can* be a changemaker. Systemic problems require big solutions—but none of that changes the fact that everyone, including people like you and me, can become powerful forces of positive change . . . if we learn to follow our fire.

Here's another way of looking at it: You are someone's answered prayer. The lie is that you have to be perfect, pretty, and put together before you can make a difference. The truth is actually the opposite. Sometimes you have to be broken and burned. You have to feel a burden. More often than not, hurt is what moves us to action. Not comfort but pain. So if you're imperfect or, better yet, if you feel a little bit of pain, welcome to the party. Pain is a primer. Pain is a preparer. Your pain, your imperfections, your sorrow, your grief, your sadness, your emotions are just what you need. The hurt adds fuel to your fire.

A good friend of mine, Jeff, is a college football

coach. He used to coach at a small school in Illinois and led his team to their first championship. That moment was special for him. But it was even more special for his dad. See, Jeff's dad had also been a coach at that same school, and though he won numerous games and set several records, the school could never manage to win a national championship. That is, until his son came along. Before Jeff became a head coach, he was the assistant to his father. He stayed by his father's side and learned the ropes. He learned the ins and outs and experienced the ups and downs. For thirteen years he felt the victories and experienced the defeats. So when my friend took over, he didn't just inherit his father's team; he inherited his father's burden, spoken or unspoken. That's why it was so special when, four years after taking over, the team—his team—won their first ever national championship. An answered prayer.

But while Jeff was answering his dad's prayer, Jeff's own son was answering his. See, before Jeff became a coach, he was a player. He was the starting quarterback on his high school team and always dreamed about playing at one of the biggest universities in the nation. Unfortunately, he never received offers from the big schools; he wasn't big enough. So he went to a smaller school. And though he achieved success at that institution, his lifelong dream to start at quarterback for a Power 5 school was never realized . . . until his son came along.

Jeff's son, Payton, spent a lot of time with his dad. He would travel to games, sit in on meetings, and even spend time in locker rooms at halftime. He was always there. So when Payton got offered a chance to play football at the small school that his dad was coaching at, you can imagine the tension that arose. Jeff let Payton decide, and a few months later, Payton made his decision. He chose to play quarterback at a Power 5 school. A few months later, after battling through homesickness and a change in coaching staff, Payton became the starting quarterback at one of the biggest colleges in the nation. An answered prayer.

You are someone's answered prayer. Your actions, your faith, your fire. All that's required is showing up. You may not be a college quarterback. You may not be a national-championship coach. You don't need to be. All you need is to get close to those around you and pay attention to your heart. Feel someone else's pain. Experience your own. Sit with it, process it, feel it. Then follow it.

There will be things in your life that make you angry. Things that make you sad. Whatever those things are, don't ignore them. Feel the pain, the sadness, the frustration, and let it remind you that you were made for more. You were meant to take your pain and turn it into purpose. Life was never meant to be easy. The American dream—two kids, a nice house—isn't the answer. It will never satisfy. What *will* satisfy is following your fire. Taking a risk. Addressing injustice. Those things that make you feel? *Feel them.* Every emotion that comes. Talk about it. Speak it out loud. Process it, whether by yourself or with people you trust and who love you. Give it to God. Ask him what you should do. Ask him where you should go.

I believe that once we discover the fire that drives us, we'll be able to heal the people and places around us. And maybe, just maybe, we'll experience healing along the way as well. Broken yet beautiful, beaten but bold.

In this book, we're going to explore how you can be a force for change in your home and community and beyond, someone who sees big problems but knows that God is bigger. And you'll find out how to identify and follow your fire—those unique passions and abilities that God has put in your heart—because that fire is the key to becoming a changemaker.

People often wonder where change starts and what the first step is. It starts on the inside, with a decision to stand up for what you believe in and to find courage in the midst of chaos. It starts with deciding that your future will be better than your past. It starts with believing that there's something worth fighting for, something worth living for. And maybe, just maybe, it's you.

But the workers are few. And change, my friends, always has and always will start with you.

ONE

BIG DREAMS
REQUIRE ARCHITECTS

love building. Not Legos or cars—I love building *people*. I love hosting people and events, and making them feel at home. That's the kind of change I have a passion for—building people up so they can unlock their potential to transform themselves and their communities. Helping them see what they were created to be.

I get that love for building from my dad. He is a doctor in mental health, a pastor, and a businessman. But beyond all of that, he's a builder whose big dreams ended up transforming an entire community. So I can't think of a better way to start this chapter than by telling you a little bit about my dad, his dream—and his architect.

A FATHER'S DREAM

The village in Nigeria where my parents are from is special. When I was little, my family and I traveled to Nigeria for Christmas and New Year's. After a day in the city, with its bustling streets and bright lights, we would go to the village, with its bumpy roads and unreliable electricity. The contrast could not have been more pronounced.

During my earliest visits to Nigeria, we stayed in my grandma's hut. One small light bulb hung from the middle of the room. It would work on occasion, but the electricity provider for the country didn't always make it to the village. When there was light we rejoiced, glad that our nights could last just a little bit longer. But usually right around 6 p.m. the electricity cut off. In the absence of electricity we learned that the stars shone a bit brighter. The sounds of creation spoke louder. But the fact remained that unreliable electricity was a real challenge for the village.

Access to water was another challenge. There was no running water in the village and no convenience stores within a forty-mile radius. If we wanted to shower, brush our teeth, or have a drink, there was one solution—the stream. It was at least a mile from the village to the stream. My mom shared stories of walking to the stream in the morning with a basket full of clothes to do laundry. Later that day she'd return to the stream with an empty five-gallon jug to get water for cooking, drinking, bathing, and brushing. Every day of the week, every week of the year. Her needs were met. But it was a hard way to live.

My dad saw the pain that his community had to go through every single day to accomplish the simplest of tasks. So he started to build. It started with a borehole. A deep dig beneath the earth's surface that provided a better—and much closer—source of water. A burden was lifted. That borehole became a beacon of hope for an entire village.

But that was only the beginning. My dad wanted this village to become a home for him and his family. He wanted to build something beautiful, something better. So, once again, he began to build. But as we all know, before you build, you need a good architect.

Thankfully, my dad had a guy.

Count the Cost

Have you ever known people who were close with your parents, but you had no idea what they did? Well, Azike Diribe was that guy for my family. Every time we went to Nigeria, he and my dad would sit, talk, plan, and scheme together. I would hear laughs, jokes, and serious conversations all happening at the kitchen table. I had no idea what they were talking about, but I was always intrigued. Mr. Diribe would usually walk in with a long, white cardboard tube filled with huge sheets of paper with some sort of drawings on them. I was too young to piece it all together, but as I grew older, I realized that those drawings were architectural plans for a magnificent home. I wondered where they were going to build it. Maybe somewhere in the big city, with the bright lights and busy streets. When I finally asked my dad, he walked me outside of the hut and pointed toward the bush. I didn't see it, but he did. He envisioned a beautiful compound with lights, running water, basketball and tennis courts, and a fountain out front. He wanted to build something that was so much more than a home—he wanted to build a multifunction compound that, like the borehole that provided water for the village, would become a source of hope and change for an entire community.

Moving from Vision to Reality

My dad's big, crazy dream eventually became a reality. The future he envisioned got charted out on those architectural blueprints that Mr. Diribe put together. And then those blueprints came to life as a beautiful building with reliable electricity and running water. It became a hub where medical missionaries and their staff could stay, bringing much-needed services to a village that had long suffered from inadequate health care.

My dad had the vision. But his architect was with him every step of the way, helping him count the cost and translate his vision into reality.

Architects listen to our dreams, refine them, and map them out. Perhaps most important, architects help us count the cost.

Do you have people like that in your life? People who believe in your dreams and don't shoot them down at first sight? People who are willing to walk with you into dark places and bring the light, or walk into dry places and bring drink? People who hear about your fire, your passion, and encourage you to follow it?

I call these people *architects*. They listen to our dreams, refine them, and map them out. Perhaps most important, architects help us count the cost.

Few things in life are free. Every dream worth building involves a cost. Time, money, influence. When an architect counts the cost, it's not to deter us from our dreams but to help us prepare for the road ahead.

TURN YOUR PASSION INTO A PLAN

A few years ago, when Colin Kaepernick began taking a knee to protest police brutality, many people were up in arms. An NFL star was protesting during the singing of the national anthem. Many fans hated him for it. Team owners weren't too pleased either. So, after a failed attempt at an ultimatum, the owners decided to issue a challenge to the players. If the players cared about making real change and were willing to put money behind it, their own money, then the league would match the players' efforts: $250,000 per year, per team. In year one our team, the Chicago Bears, raised nearly $1 million. With help from players, coaches, staff, fans, and a few different NFL grants, the city of Chicago saw a huge influx of attention and resources. But that was just the beginning.

LISTEN AND LEARN

After the devastating murder of George Floyd, I decided to bring some people together, people who do not normally interact: Mitch Trubisky, Allen Robison, Jonathan Toews, Malcolm Subban, Jason Heyward, Jason Kipnis, Ryan Arcidiacono, Max Strus, Tyler Lancaster, and Austin Carr. For those who don't know these names, they are players from the Chicago Bears, Chicago Bulls, Chicago Cubs, Chicago Blackhawks, and Northwestern graduates who play pro sports. Along with Brittany Payton, daughter of Chicago Bears great Walter Payton; Diamond DeShields, all-star guard for the Chicago Sky; and Lucas Giolito, all-star pitcher for the Chicago White Sox, we came together. We showed up from different teams and different sports in hopes of making a difference in one city: Chicago.

We all wanted to do something, but we didn't know

what. We had passion but needed a plan. Should we protest? Post on social media? Preach to anyone who was willing to hear? Or listen and learn? Though all those options seemed viable to effect change, we chose the last one—listening and learning. We sat down with kids from the South and West sides of Chicago and just listened. We invited police officers so they could listen as well. And what we heard was telling. We heard thirteen-year-old girls air out their grievances with the police. Wondering why so many altercations between law enforcement and Black people turned violent. We heard fifteen-year-old boys who were certain that things would never change. We heard a lot. But what we saw was even more telling. While on a bus tour of the Austin neighborhood on the West Side of Chicago—a trip meant to show the players the devastation of the rioting and looting—we *saw* hopelessness. We saw a neighborhood that the government, the police, and the entire society had turned their backs on. A people forgotten.

Gathering my friends and colleagues who had a heart for helping the city of Chicago was a first step. An important step. We all had a desire to bring change. But we needed to channel that passion into a plan. Listening and simply being present with the people in our city who were hurting the most helped us identify the need. And ultimately, a vision started to take shape. It wouldn't be long before we would need to find our architects.

GET READY

I'm going to share more in the chapters ahead about how we transformed our passion into a plan to address the problem of the food desert on Chicago's West Side. But right now I want to ask you to look in your own heart for a moment. Do you have a dream? A vision for your family, community, or city? What problems do you see that need to be solved? You may be thinking, *My dream is too expensive, too unrealistic. I've counted the cost and I just can't afford it.* Before you give up on your dream, remind yourself of your vision. Close your eyes and imagine all that you hope to create. All that you desire to see. Overwhelm your fear with the vision. Believe. Don't doubt. Constantly remind yourself of where you want to go.

How many of us are afraid to dream? We think we're not worthy enough to hold such a precious idea. We think it'll never work. We think joy, peace, and a firm foundation are reserved for someone else on a different side of town, with a white picket fence and nice

You'll need to listen and
learn, sit with people who
are suffering, discover
how your passion can
get channeled into
something that'll make
a real difference.

family pictures. We think they've got it figured out and that we're best off lying low and living with the hand we're dealt. I disagree with that notion. I want you to open your eyes and see all that's in front of you. See through the fog and recognize that hope is coming— and you might be the one who's bringing it.

And so many dreams die before they become a reality because we get stuck at the vision phase. You're responsible to find your dream and nourish it. You'll need to listen and learn, sit with people who are suffering, discover how your passion can get channeled into something that'll make a real difference. But at some point, you're going to need an architect.

If we want to accomplish big things, we need people who will help bring our dreams to life. People who hear about our fire, our passion, and encourage us to follow it. Good architects listen to our dreams, refine them, and map them out. And they help us count the cost— not to deter us from our dreams but to help us prepare for the road ahead.

I should also share a warning: Some people are the opposite of architects. They want to tear you down. When you want to go further in life, don't listen to negative voices. The ones within or the ones without. Eliminate them from your life. Whether that means blocking some people on social media or in real life,

you owe them nothing. You owe your dream everything. You have that vision for a reason, but so many
people will try to quiet you down, shut you out, and
keep you from speaking up. Why? I don't know. But
what I do know is that they don't have the vision. You
do. So keep on dreaming, dreamer. Keep on believing,
believer. Keep on building.

My son Kelechi is four years old. He is full of energy
and never stops moving. I jokingly gave him the nick-
name Energy because he'll be up at five in the morning
jumping up and down, running, playing, and letting off
steam. Like I said, energy. He is full of it. If his energy is
not pointed in the right direction, he will destroy everything. But when directed in the right way, Kelechi is a
builder. He's a problem solver. He'll spend hours working on a single project. He wants to master it. "No, I
wanna do it myself" is probably his favorite phrase. But
he needs us, his parents, to give him a plan and help
him stick to it. So for all the architects out there—the
moms of energetic kids, the wives or husbands of energetic spouses—we need you. We need you more than
you can imagine.

One of my architects has been my counselor. I tell
him what's going on in my life and he listens. He offers
suggestions and helps me make the situation better. It's
still my dream, but my architect helps it go from dream

to reality. I have other friends who are architects too. Brett and Boomer, Lukas and Steve. My brother too. These men encourage me. They build me up when I'm broken down. They remind me of God's plan even when things go awry. All these individuals help me count the cost and do the important work of a dreamer and builder.

People often talk about change in ways that make it seem far off and out of reach. They believe that being a changemaker is reserved for the few, the talented, the gifted. I would push back on that notion. I would say that anyone can bring positive change. You just need a good idea and a little bit of help. Don't ever be afraid to ask for help. Don't be afraid to ask for an architect.

I've been afraid before. Even as I write this book, I'm fighting with feelings of fear and inadequacy. I'm afraid of the journey but eager to get to the destination. I'm afraid that I'll miss something along the way. That I'll be hurt or take a wrong step. That I won't pick up what I was supposed to or that I'll change into something or someone I don't want to be.

Fear is a real emotion, but it's not always honest. It's often based on a lie or, better said, a distorted sense of reality or sense of self. When the fear kicks in, I call on my architects. Those around me who know me best. These are people who know the vision and are committed to help me accomplish it, people who I've trusted with my dreams and remind me that life is, in fact, a journey. These people are few and far between, but they are essential for anyone who wants to dream and build something worthwhile.

If you're afraid, flood the fear with vision. And be on the lookout for your architects.

TWO

THE POWER OF
PERSPECTIVE

As much as I hate to admit it, I care a lot about what people think of me.

I'm learning to change that. I'm learning that if I want to make a change and create as big of an impact as possible, I need to put my ego aside and stop caring about what people think. I need to remember that people's opinions don't matter and that I'm being prideful when I focus on how people perceive me.

Pride is simply thinking about yourself too much, and that's why being overly concerned with other people's perceptions is really a form of pride. Beyond that, focusing on what others think can result in me not using all of my gifts and instead hiding them. The more I hide, the less I'm able to let my light shine. There's a great example of this in the Bible. Matthew, one of Jesus' followers, recorded some of Jesus' words as he was speaking to a crowd. "You are the salt of the earth, but if salt has lost its taste, how shall its saltiness be restored? It is no longer good for anything except to be thrown out and trampled under people's feet."[1]

That's pretty intense. But it made me think. My oldest son, Caleb, loves seasoning. He's in a phase now where he wants to put pepper on everything. But if salt, or pepper for that matter, did not season the food, it would be useless. It would not accomplish the very thing it was made to do. You are salt.

But Jesus doesn't stop there. He continued, "You are the light of the world. A city that is set on a hill cannot be hidden. Nor do they light a lamp and put it under a basket, but on a lampstand, and it gives light to all who are in the house. Let your light so shine before men, that they may see your good works and glorify your Father in heaven."[2]

SALT AND LIGHT

It was December of 2021, and I had just started my new job at ESPN. I was on the field, standing next to the end zone for my first time ever as a field analyst, when my phone rang. I picked it up. It was my wife, Ngozi.

"How are you doing?" she greeted me.

"Doing great, Babe."

I wasn't, really. But I didn't want her to know that. I hadn't been able to analyze the game; it felt like the people I was working with weren't letting me talk! I was down on the field watching everything unfold, but my mic was off and they rarely turned it on. I was frustrated.

Being a field analyst is great. The only issue is, you're by yourself on the field while your partners are together in the booth. Because of that, they'll often put your mic on mute unless you have a specific comment. And then, if you get a chance, it's not long before you're back on mute. For a guy who loves to talk, this was extremely frustrating—torturous, almost! It wasn't just torture because I love to talk but because I felt I had some great insight to share, not only from playing the game for nearly two decades but also from my position on the field. I was so close to the players one time that I celebrated a touchdown with the team! I was on the field, behind the bench, next to the players, listening in on coaches' conversations. I had so much insight, but I didn't know how to get it out. That was when my wife's call came through.

Usually I wouldn't pick up a phone call during work, but my entire family had just left for a trip to Nigeria and I was waiting for them to land. Plus, I wasn't getting chances to comment on the game anyway, so I decided to pick up. The connection was bad, but it stayed connected just long enough for me to say hi to everyone and to see my daughter, Sophia, full of joy. They had made it; they were fine. But I wasn't. I was in a new role at a new job with little to no opportunity.

Usually stadiums don't have good cell service,

especially midway through a big game. But for whatever reason, this call came through. And though it was spotty, I did catch one last thing before the call dropped. The last thing I heard my wife say was, "Have fun."

It was a simple truth that many of us often forget. I had to ask her to repeat it because I wanted to make sure I heard her right. This was my first game, and millions of people were watching. It was a big deal. Also, many of the other games had been canceled, so this was the only game being broadcast. Plus it was around Christmas, so everyone was off work. In a lot of ways, it should have been a high-pressure situation. And in a lot of ways, I was treating it as such. Though I'm extremely effusive, I didn't want to talk *too* much. I didn't want to step on anyone's toes, I didn't want to overdo it. So much was on the line. But after a quarter and a half, I wasn't happy. I wasn't having fun. I wasn't getting to be me.

So that call and my wife's words freed me. They reminded me of what really matters. They reminded me of who I am. She helped build me up. After that call, everything changed. I forgot about the audience and the audio issues and whether I was getting enough opportunities to talk—and I decided to have fun. I'm so glad I picked up the phone that day.

It might sound strange, but my wife's reminder to

have fun also reminded me of something else: how the fear of God sets you free from every other fear. When you fear God, you stop fearing people. When you fear God, you're focused on what he thinks and you stop caring what anyone else thinks. When you fear God, all other fear goes out the window.

Fearing God means honoring him. It means trusting him. It doesn't mean being afraid; it's realizing that he is big, he is real, and he is worth our time and attention.

When I picked up that call from my wife, it brought a change in perspective. And that change in perspective changed me. It reminded me of who I was. I remembered that as a God-fearer, I didn't need to fear anything else. And I felt free to embrace the joy of the moment.

No matter who has put you on mute, no matter who's trying to prevent you from going to the places that you want to go, no matter what obstacles are in your way, you have a choice. You *always* have a choice. You can choose to see things the way everyone else sees them, or you can choose to have fun. Choose to change your situation or at least your perspective of your situation. Choose to get close. Choose to change your perspective. Better yet, choose to let your perspective change you. Perspective is everything.

I chose a perspective that day, a different perspective than I may have chosen in the past. I chose to forget

When you fear God, you're focused on what he thinks and you stop caring what anyone else thinks. When you fear God, all other fear goes out the window.

about the people who were watching, to forget about the people in my ear who wouldn't let me speak. I decided to have fun. The rest of the game was a breeze. I almost forgot I had a mic. I was standing inches from the end zone where the action happened and found myself celebrating on the field with the players who did the work. See, you don't have to be on the team to celebrate, but you do have to make a choice. My sole purpose was to have fun. Everything else emanated from there. And that emanation led to a culmination.

CHOOSE THE UNSTUCK PERSPECTIVE

As the game ended, I was asked to interview the player of the game, Taulia Tagovailoa. Lia is a rare talent. He's a star QB who had just led his team to a near fifty-point victory. But before I could interview him, before I could ask him any questions, he recognized me. I found him on the field and we began catching up while I waited for my cameraman. Lia—the quarterback of the team, the MVP, the future NFL star—looked at me and said, "I've seen you before. I saw you yesterday. You were on ESPN."

Even when you don't think you're letting your light shine, it's shining. Even if you don't believe you are being salt and light to the world, you are. So keep it up. Keep on going. Keep on dreaming, building, and believing.

When my perspective shifted midway through that game, I started focusing on the joy of the moment. I thought I was stuck on the sidelines with no opportunity to shine, but I wasn't—and neither are you. You have a choice. You *always* have a choice. It may not be easy. It may not be obvious, but it's there. When I chose to have fun, I stopped caring if I was going to get to talk on TV again. I decided to live in the moment. That decision changed everything.

Moments after interviewing Lia, I met a man named John who added even more fuel to my fire. Out of nowhere he approached me and said, "You're doing great work, dude. Your passion, your joy, your authenticity—it's so palpable. I saw you running from sideline to sideline, making sure you're in the right spot. Keep up the great work—I love it." I asked John what he did for a living. He told me that he travels all around the country. His job: to bring heated benches to stadiums for cold games. Follow the fire.

Have fun. Choose joy. Choose the perspective that you have options, even if you feel stuck. When you find that perspective, you'll be amazed at how things start to open up around you. Opportunities. Unexpected words of encouragement from others. It takes you from merely doing a job and puts you into the game.

And it didn't end there! Friends from years back saw the game and commented on it. Their texts made me smile. They told me that they had been following my journey and that they were proud of what I had accomplished. And then I got a text from Adam Eaton. He's an all-star baseball player but an even better human being. Eight years earlier, when I was doing a radio show at a sports bar on my day off from the NFL, Adam had been one of my guests. Now he was watching me be a field analyst for the worldwide leader in sports. He witnessed my journey from Native New Yorker bar to New York Yankee Stadium.

CHOOSE THE CONFIDENT PERSPECTIVE

Early in my college football career, confidence was not my thing. I would second-guess myself all the time. It got to a point where my coaches noticed. They gave me a challenge. "Sam," one coach said, "I want you to practice trusting your gut. Practice trusting your instincts. You're the one on the field. You have information and intel that I don't. Trust your gut and report back to me what happens."

I was floored. I didn't know that you could practice confidence. I didn't realize that it was a skill that could be acquired. But it turns out my coach was right. Every day in practice, I tried trusting my gut and believing what I sensed. And nine times out of ten I would guess right. Even when I guessed wrong, I was able to recover more quickly. This newfound confidence changed my game completely. And it can change yours too.

Have you labeled yourself a people pleaser? Remind yourself that you are not a people pleaser. In your past you've had people-pleasing tendencies, but you can change. Have you told yourself you're not smart enough? Tell yourself a new story: You are not unintelligent. You have just made some bad decisions in your past. Make new choices. Practice new habits. I'm telling you, it works. You can change your habits. You can change your negative mind-sets. You can change your family and your community. Just try it. Practice it. Tell me how it works. Change starts with you.

If I'd never taken my coach's advice and accepted that challenge, I never would have known the confidence that existed on the other side. On the other side of risk. On the other side of a question. On the other side of action. On the other side of showing up.

A few months later, people began to notice. Not only on the field but also off of it. I was speaking at a men's conference later that year, and after I spoke one of the attendees approached me. "Excuse me, sir," he began. "How did you get so confident?"

I was floored. I looked at him, shocked by what he had seen in me. Surprised that he was using that word to describe me.

"I've never been called that before," I said. "But I'm honored. And I'm learning to trust my gut every day."

This man had seen something in me that I had never seen in myself. He saw who I'd become. Those decisions I made to trust my instincts were the building blocks for a real change in who I was. Choose to see yourself as confident, capable, and equipped for the things God has called you to do. It'll make a difference in your life and empower you to make a difference in the lives of others.

CHOOSE THE FAITH PERSPECTIVE

In 2013 I suffered a season-ending injury. I was playing for the Arizona Cardinals and had broken my leg in the third game of the season. I was devastated, but I wasn't crushed. I believed that God would turn my pain into purpose. I had a good friend who believed the same. Yes, there were times of doubt and of pain, but my friend reminded me not to waste my suffering.

"Sam," he began, "you love people. You love spending time with them and seeing the best in them. You also love speaking and being on camera. Why not reach out to a local TV station, tell them who you are, and tell them what you want to do?"

So I did. When football, the thing I loved the most, was taken away from me, I found a new love. I exercised a new muscle. I was on a scooter and I couldn't walk, but I could talk. And boy, did I love to talk. My local TV station started a weekly segment called *Sam in the City*. I would go to the studio and practice speaking to the camera, working with anchors, and developing content. I'll never forget my first meeting with Jill Hanks. She was the NBC executive who gave me my first shot on TV. I had written a blog called *From Field to Fan* and sent it to her. I guess that's where I realized my love for writing as well. I wrote a lot that year after suffering a major injury for the first time in my life. I had more time to think. I was less busy, less distracted. I was at peace.

A majority of my first book, *Let the World See You*, was also written in a time of pretty intense pain. I had just torn my left pectoral muscle. I was out for another season, and once again I found purpose through my pain. It was during that time that I discovered my love for serving people and convening resources for those who didn't have access on their own. I was living in Chicago and felt a deep desire to help people in the community in a more meaningful way. I was tired of people brushing off the violence and death in Black communities. I was also tired of seeing no one in public office or public service doing anything about it. Police officers are meant to serve and protect, but it seemed some areas were being overlooked. You can imagine my surprise when I found out that some police officers actually avoided certain neighborhoods that had a lot of illegal activity. *Isn't this what you were hired to stop?* I thought. I was angry.

The truth is, you can't follow the fire until you find the flame. And you may not find the fire until you're forced to look. When I broke my leg, I was left with a choice. I could choose to sulk or choose to start looking for what God might have next for me. I chose the latter. And it was at that point that I realized football was just a platform for me to do the things I *really* loved to do: speak, write, and lead and encourage others. Football was a vehicle for the flames, but it was not the fire itself.

Think of a car. A car gets you from point A to point B, but the engine is what makes it go. Your fire is like the engine of a car. It's the same for people. You're going somewhere. So am I. We may look different and have different dreams, but we both need something to keep us going. We need a fire.

I first fell in love with TV and writing through what

seemed like a tragedy. Experiencing an injury derailed my football season, but it was that season of pain and disappointment that helped me discover what I really loved. My first steps toward discovering and following my fire were small, but eventually I found myself writing bestselling books and working for ESPN, the worldwide leader in sports. From *First Take* to the Fiesta Bowl, from calling games to creating content, I was there. Why? Because I chose to turn my pain into purpose.

Moving from pain to purpose is never easy. In fact, I don't think it's possible without the right perspective. We talked about the perspective shift I had as a new field analyst with ESPN. Choosing not to feel stuck and deciding to find joy in the moment totally transformed my experience that day and opened up some amazing opportunities. But there's an even deeper perspective shift that unlocks our ability to have hope, even when we're in the middle of a painful, difficult circumstance: a faith perspective.

There's a story in the Bible about two blind men. You've probably heard it before, but there's one specific part you may not have noticed. In this story Jesus was traveling to Jerusalem when two blind men heard him walking by and cried out for help, but the crowd told them to be quiet. The crowd put them on mute.

But when Jesus saw the blind men, he felt compassion for them.

Even though I'm not blind, I can identify with these two men. I've been in their shoes—ignored or silenced in my moment of need. I'm sure you have too. I don't know what I would have done in that situation. After being shushed, I may not have wanted to speak up. I may have listened to the crowd. Thankfully, these guys didn't. These blind men had the kind of courage that comes only from faith.

"Lord!" they shouted. "Have mercy on us!"[3]

He did. That moment was the moment everything changed. They faced their fear and chose faith. They believed Jesus could help them, so when the crowd told them to shut up, they *spoke up* even louder. These men, these brave, blind beggars, got Jesus' attention.

There will always be noise. There will always be doubters and detractors telling you to quiet down and speak less. Don't listen. Don't let them put your fire out. In fact, do the opposite. Talk louder. Be effusive, loquacious, verbose. Miracles just might happen.

Jesus went on to heal these men, but not until he asked them what they wanted: "Jesus stopped and called them. 'What do you want me to do for you?' he asked. 'Lord,' they answered, 'we want our sight.'"[4]

I'm learning that before you can see what's in front

There will always be noise. There will always be doubters and detractors telling you to quiet down and speak less. Don't listen. Don't let them put your fire out.

of you, you have to make a decision. You have to make a big, bold, brave decision to have faith like a blind man. Sometimes God has to slow you down so you can see what he's doing. And other times you have to slow him down, calling out with bold faith and telling him about your deepest hope or your biggest dream.

Will you choose the perspective of faith? The perspective to look past all the things that make you feel stuck? Do you have the faith to speak up when you've been told to shut up?

If you do, it can change everything.

THREE

DREAMS ARE
CONTAGIOUS

recently read the biblical story of Nehemiah. He was a man who followed the fire. Nehemiah was the cup-bearer to King Artaxerxes of Persia. He wasn't in the highest position; he was a helper, a trusted assistant to the ruler. He wasn't the king, but he was close to him. Kings have power and influence that can make others jealous. And jealousy can lead to foul play. So before the king drank or ate, Nehemiah was there to taste everything first, risking his life as a service to the king. In addition to tasting any food or drink that the king was to consume, a cupbearer's role also included serving as the king's trusted advisor. Because of his proximity, Nehemiah was privy to private conversations and the king turned to him for sound wisdom.

Have you ever heard a piece of news and knew you needed to do something about it? Have you read something online and had your heart sink? Have you received a call from a loved one and didn't know how to respond?

Nehemiah knew the king well. But he also knew something else: his city was in need. He was from Jerusalem, but he was working in Persia. At the time,

Nehemiah's people, the Jews, were mostly living in exile, having been conquered and taken captive many years earlier. But some had returned from exile to Jerusalem and discovered that the walls of their beloved city had been destroyed.

When Nehemiah heard the news, he was devastated. What stood out to me most about this account was his immediate response. Before he sprang into action, before he saved the day, before he did anything of value, he wept. Nehemiah mourned the loss.

"When I heard these words, I sat down and wept and mourned for days; and I was fasting and praying before the God of heaven."[1] Before Nehemiah made any sort of move, he had to process his emotions. He was sad. Not for a moment, but for days. Sometimes sadness is a prerequisite to success. Just like pain can lead you to your purpose, it can also be a precedent to progress. After Nehemiah wept, mourned, fasted, and prayed, he approached the king with a plan.

There's an important lesson here—a principle we can follow: if we want to accomplish anything of significance in this world, we must feel the pain of the people and be courageous enough to have a conversation with those in positions of power.

I regularly pray for courage. Sometimes I still want to run away. But I ask myself, *If I stay, what will*

Sometimes sadness
is a prerequisite to
success. Just like
pain can lead you to
your purpose, it can
also be a precedent
to progress.

happen? What breakthrough could occur in my life and in the lives of others?

NEHEMIAH MOMENTS

My Nehemiah moment came when I raised some concerns with Roger Goodell, the commissioner of the NFL. We got to know each other after spending a year or so negotiating a new collective bargaining agreement between the NFL and the NFL Players Association. But that's not how we became close. We became close through my courageous response to an inconspicuous text.

In June 2020 George McCaskey and I made a video addressing racial inequalities in America. George is the chairman of the Chicago Bears. I was a player for the team. George was in management. I was in the union. George is white. I am Black. We have stark differences on the outside. But we care deeply about a lot of the same things. Inspired by a famous Richard Pryor and Chevy Chase skit from a 1975 episode of *Saturday Night Live*, George and I decided to share a short video that we filmed together, in which we illustrated how two people from vastly different backgrounds and perspectives can come together and find common ground. A few days after sharing the video, I received a text from a number that I didn't recognize.

> Sam, I just saw the video with George. It was powerful. Thank you for doing this.—RG

I was glad to receive the text, and excited that people were being impacted by the video. But the sign-off confused me. I didn't know who RG was, and I didn't know too many people who signed off with their initials. So I responded as honestly as I knew how.

> Thanks so much. I don't have this number saved; can you share it so I can lock it in?

> Sam. It is Roger G. Sorry if that was confusing.

I was still confused. But after a few minutes of scrolling through my mental Rolodex of possible names, I decided that this must be Roger Goodell since I don't know too many other Roger Gs—especially ones who know the chairman of the Chicago Bears on a first-name basis. I nearly responded with a simple thank-you and moved on, but I decided against it. I recognized that this text provided a Nehemiah type of opportunity. It was time for me to exercise some courage, to step out in faith.

So I responded as boldly and confidently as I knew how. Thanks so much, Roger. Would love to have a conversation about ways to make the game better . . . and more diverse.

People say that you miss 100 percent of the shots you don't take. So I took my shot, and by the grace of God, it went in.

For sure, Roger responded. Let me know when.

A little less than a week later, I was on a Zoom call with the commissioner of the National Football League. That call took place on Jason Heyward's yacht. For those of you who don't know that name, Jason plays with the Chicago Cubs and he's a World Series Champion. My life is crazy. I have no idea how I end up in some of the situations that I do. The only answer is that more often than not, I follow the fire. I walk through the open doors in front of me, even if I don't know what's on the other side.

Following the fire means taking a risk. It means facing your fear. It means addressing issues in your life that you have ignored. It means showing up and showing yourself off to the world. Not your filtered images— your*self*. The real you. Chase the passion. Notice the fear, address it, and fight to get past it. No matter how long it takes. That's what I'm working toward, and I hope that if this book does anything, it'll inspire you to do the same. Because when you follow the fire, crazy things will happen and opportunities will open up in front of you. So before I tell you about my conversation with RG, let me tell you how I ended up on Jason's yacht in the first place. It all started with listening circles.

WHEN OPPORTUNITY KNOCKS

I was first introduced to listening circles when my Chicago Bears teammates and I wanted to make an impact in the city that we called home, but we didn't know how. We wanted to *act*, not just talk. We wanted to change our community. When I first heard about the idea of listening circles, I was less than impressed. But I figured we'd give it a try. I'm glad we did.

A listening circle, according to the National Association of Community and Restorative Justice, is "an alternative process of communication, based on traditional discussion and healing practices of aboriginal peoples in Canada and the Southwestern United States."[2] Sometimes called a "peacemaking circle," it's a process that brings people together who wish to "engage in conflict resolution, healing, support, decision making or other activities when honest communications, relationship development, and community building are desired outcomes. . . . Circles [create] trust, respect, intimacy, goodwill, belonging, generosity, mutuality and reciprocity."[3] Everyone in the circle is equal, decisions are made by consensus, and everyone agrees to abide by guidelines established by the group based on shared values. Regardless of the type, the goal of a circle is simple: to provide a safe space, a sacred space, for people to grow. And we did.

There were a handful of us initially: two players, five kids, and one trained circle keeper. This circle keeper, who also happened to be a former city of Chicago police officer, had a unique role. Her job was to set the tone of the gathering, to build trust between members of the group, and to balance everyone's interests and perspectives. Our group met every week for the next month. Same circle, same community. We learned, grew, and changed together.

I have found myself in a few more listening circles since then. I've gathered with politicians and pro athletes, Super Bowl champions and superintendents of the Chicago Police Department, kids and commissioners of pro sports leagues. Everyone was equal. Honest communication, no logos, and no egos. Sharing our grievances, sharing our hearts.

In chapter 1 I shared how in the summer of 2020, I was part of a group of athletes that wanted to help heal our city. After spending time in listening circles with kids living on the West Side of Chicago and cops who worked in the neighborhood, I boarded a bus along with nine other pro athletes. We wanted to see what the situation looked like up close and personal, so we took a tour of the West Side. What we saw was devastating.

Plywood panels covered nearly every window. Broken glass was everywhere. The community had been boarded up to protect their buildings from looters and squatters. Let me say this: I do not condone destruction, but I understand it. Frustration that results in destruction is a way to process your unresolved anger. These are the same emotions that lead people to destroy friendships, break up marriages, or tear down business relationships. I believe that this destruction complex comes from unprocessed emotions and unaddressed issues. When we fail to address what is causing us pain or frustration, the result is outbursts at friends and loved ones—or the destruction of our own communities. Both are coping mechanisms that cause destruction, but some types of destruction are more visible than others.

I was deeply grieved by the brokenness I saw. But my sadness had less to do with broken glass and more to do with a broken system. Broken glass can be swept up. A broken system takes a lot more time to fix. I'm reminded of Ephesians 6:10–13, a passage about how our battle is not against flesh and blood but against powers and spiritual forces of evil. Sounds creepy but it's true. There's a bigger battle we're fighting. We pray, "Thy kingdom come, thy will be done in earth, as it is in heaven."[4] What would it look like for the kingdom of God to come here on earth? We have an opportunity to be a part of building God's kingdom. But sometimes part of the building process involves a battle that we need to fight. And we can't fight it alone.

As we drove through the community, I noticed Jason Heyward was sitting by the window on the right side of the bus, staring out at the city that he had called home. Jason isn't just a great baseball player, he's a hero to many people in Chicago. He helped lead the Chicago Cubs to their first World Series win in over a century. It's easy for people with Jason's level of achievement and popularity to stay in their bubbles and avoid things that could hurt them. But that's not who Jason is, and in this moment, it was clear that something was happening in his heart. Something was clicking for him. I could see it. So I decided to ask a question.

"J," I began. "We've been on this bus for a while now. Can I ask you a question?"

"Sure," he replied.

"How many grocery stores have you seen in this neighborhood?"

"Maybe one," he said.

"How many liquor stores have you seen?"

"Over ten," he responded.

"That's a problem," I said.

He agreed. His response would lead to a renewed purpose for both of us. A fire identifier. A pain point. An issue that we saw but didn't exactly know what to do with. Soon we would learn.

The Food Desert

Have you ever heard of the term *food desert*? It's a region where grocery stores are scarce and liquor stores are a dime a dozen. That's what Jason and I saw on that bus ride through Chicago. I was familiar with the concept because of what I observed and experienced when I was a kid growing up in Texas.

I love food. I don't think I'm alone in that! But when I was a kid, I noticed that certain foods, in certain neighborhoods, were more readily available than others. I noticed how unhealthy foods such as highly processed snacks, donuts, and sodas were cheaper and more accessible in the Black neighborhoods that I frequented than they were in white ones. I noticed that the opposite was true for healthy foods.

As a kid, I thought this phenomenon was specific to the area I grew up in. You see, I lived in two different worlds. Early in my childhood, I went to school on the south side of Dallas. My Sunday and Wednesday nights were spent there as well. My dad was a pastor of a church in this predominantly Black neighborhood, so whenever we were there at a gas station or a grocery store, I would see that apples cost $3 (if they were available at all), while donuts were $0.25. Oranges were $2.75 and cinnamon rolls were $0.50 each. Something didn't add up.

I loved sweets, so I didn't complain. I was glad that my measly dollar could buy so many tasty treats. But something about that experience felt wrong. I had been learning in school, at home, and even on TV about the importance of eating healthy. How it leads to longer life and better health. But this didn't make sense. There was a plethora of unhealthy foods in the poor neighborhoods, but the rich neighborhoods, like the one where I would later go to school, were flooded with healthy food options. I was shocked.

But I came to realize that this wasn't only true for the neighborhoods I grew up in; it was true for neighborhoods in other parts of the country as well, and all around the world. A subtle but startling reminder of injustice. And it was on full display during that bus ride through Chicago.

The conversation that stood out to me the most from

that bus ride was a statement made not by a pro athlete but by a teenager. Azariah is a fifteen-year-old phenom. She's smart, funny, and brilliant beyond measure. Her long black braids stood as a crown on her head. Her vocabulary would put any Harvard grad to shame. The other athletes and I were touring the West Side, but this was Azariah's neighborhood. We were preparing to return to our comfortable houses in safe communities. But Azariah lived in this food desert. And she decided to make sure we remembered it. "You all see this as a field trip," she said. "But some of us choose to live here. We call this place home. I hope you'll remember that when you go back to your homes."

As we rode through those neighborhoods, I felt as if we were in a developing country like Nigeria. Dirt roads, underdeveloped. It didn't make sense. One side of the street was beautiful, while the other had been abandoned. The government had turned its back on a community. I was angry. Jason was angry. Everyone on that bus was angry. But as we all know, anger is a secondary emotion. Underneath that anger resided sadness and despair.

The athletes on that bus lived in neighborhoods with government support and sufficient resources. We had no idea such devastation existed in our city. That's why it's good to get close.

And after witnessing our shock at what we were see-ing, Azariah spoke. She spoke the truth to the people who could do something about it. What exactly could we do? She wasn't sure about that yet. But what she did know is that we showed up. We cared. And because we cared, she decided to share her care with a few new friends.

We *heard* her.

When Jason and I left that day, we weren't sure what to do next. We had different ideas, but we were united in our desire to create change. A few days later, I got a text from Jason.

Wzup bro. I'm getting together with some of the cops we met in those circles from the other day. Let me know if you wanna come through.

I did. But I didn't know what to expect. I had just met Jason, and now he was asking me to come hang out with him, some cops, and a few friends. Plus, it was the same day I was supposed to meet with RG! But I had committed, so I showed up.

When I reached the address Jason had given me, there were no houses, no apartments, just a building next to some water. I was confused. I walked about two laps around the place, and even typed the address into a different search engine to make sure I had it right.

Finally I parked on the street and called Jason to let him know I was there.

"Oh yeah, just come to the back," he said. "Behind the building."

All I saw was the lake and some boats and a dock with a walkway. I kept on walking up and down the dock, looking for the restaurant that I assumed must be behind one of those buildings since he had asked for my food order. As I walked down the dock, I saw some people on a boat and realized that was the location the GPS was leading me to. Still confused, I texted Jason once again. I'm in the back, bro.

I see you. I'll have my guy come get you.

As I stood there, a sturdy, bald Italian guy walked down the dock toward me.

"Acho," he said. "Come this way. J's waiting on you."

Turns out, we were meeting on Jason's boat. Waiting there was Jason, his assistant, and two of the cops I had met just days earlier. Except this time they weren't in uniform, and we weren't in circles. We were all casually hanging out on Jason's boat. All equal, no power structures. Jason has a way of creating that environment for people.

Upon boarding the boat, we began our voyage. We

talked, we laughed, we got to know one another. We listened to the police officers' stories and exchanged experiences. We got close. But in the back of my mind, I knew I had to leave soon to be on time for my Zoom call with RG.

When I told Jason that I needed to head out and shared the reason why, he responded, "You can make the call here." But I didn't want to risk it. I was sure I needed to get this boat back to the dock and get my butt back to the car. I had another hour drive ahead of me, and knowing Chicago traffic, I didn't want to be late.

Jason directed the helmsman back to the dock and I began to pack up my stuff. "You sure you don't wanna stay, bro?" he said again. "I got Wi-Fi here, I got a room downstairs you can use too. Your choice, but I don't want you to feel rushed trying to make the drive."

I was skeptical. This Zoom call with Roger was important, and the idea of relying on the Wi-Fi on a boat made me really nervous! But by this time I knew there was no way I was going to make it home and I'd have to find a place to stop and make the call on the way. I offered up a prayer, turned to Jason, and said, "You know what, J? I'll stay. Where's that room you talked about?"

He was excited. Not necessarily because I was staying, but because he was leading. He was causing me to believe in possibilities, just like he had done with his team. We all need friends like J. We all need leaders like him too. People who believe when we don't.

The call with RG went great. We talked for about an hour about life, football, and ways to make change in the community. Sometimes we need to get close. Prior to that call, I had no way of knowing how much Roger Goodell, the commissioner of the NFL, actually cared about the issues that I cared about. But now I know just how deeply he cares about people, fighting injustice, and finding solutions. He cares about making lasting change. I learned all of that from getting close.

I was recently at the library with my son. He's seven years old and can touch the top of my head. He's a big kid. While standing about ten yards away from me, he stuck his hand out in front of his face. "Daddy!" he exclaimed. "My hand can cover your whole body from back there. But from here it seems different. It can't even cover your face." He went back and tried it again. He was amazed. From far away, people and things seem so much smaller than they actually are. But when you get close, your perspective changes. I would never have known that had I not responded to that text from RG. I would never have known that had I not gotten close.

It turns out that RG not only wanted to *talk* about change but also to *be* about change. He had been having constant conversations with guys around the league and experts in the field about ways to make change. So I started sharing my hope to make a difference in Chicago.

Listen and Learn

Over the next four weeks we hosted four more listening circles with developers, planners, architects, and athletes. We knew there were too many liquor stores and too few grocery stores. We knew that this broken-down community needed to be built up. So we were going to build something together.

Conversation is the way. Listening is the key. I felt pretty certain that finding a way to bring healthy food options to this community was the right step for us to take. But when we had the idea of building a food mart on the West Side, it was just that: an idea. We needed to know if the kids would be involved. We needed to know if it was what they *wanted*. So we asked. We shared what we saw (the abundance of liquor stores and the single grocery store) and asked about their experience. We asked where their food came from and if they would even want a food mart in their community. The responses startled us.

"Sam," one of the kids said, "if we want to get something healthy, something organic, we have to commute forty-five minutes to the next city for that. So yes, we would *love* a food mart in our community." With that question, with that conversation, the journey began. Athletes continued to show up. So did the kids. So did the architects. Week after week, day after day, we planned, played, and prayed together. We dreamed together. In just four weeks we'd raised half a million dollars.

It was truly a Nehemiah moment. Nehemiah built something too. After crying and talking with the king, Nehemiah went back to Jerusalem to survey the damage. He inspected the walls and gathered his people to rebuild them. It took just fifty-two days for Nehemiah and his people to rebuild the wall in Jerusalem.[5]

Like Nehemiah, we wanted to rebuild our torn-down community. Like Nehemiah, mourning preceded our action. I had mourned—mourned *deeply*—in the days and weeks since the death of George Floyd. But then I acted. Like Nehemiah, I talked to powerful allies. And I'm telling you, there's something about momentum that moves a dream into the realm of reality. Four weeks after our initial meeting, we held the first liquor store teardown party. I invited Roger G. He showed up. Seven weeks after that, the Austin Harvest pop-up food mart would be built.

Do you believe in miracles?

When something catches fire, it's hard to put out.

And we had caught fire. We were on fire for this project. Raising the money proved to be an easy task, as did getting people to show up. What was more difficult was believing that this was even real. The pop-up mart was built, but the kids wanted a more permanent structure that could be open year-round. So we had to start building again.

The pop-up mart was open three days a week: Monday, Wednesday, and Friday from 2 to 6 p.m. It was an open-air, fresh-food market. And while it was special, we knew it was temporary. We opened the facility in August and, living in Chicago, we knew that winter was coming and the open-air, pop-up mart would have to shut down. We didn't want that. After a few weeks of work, the kids were in love. They fell in love with the work, they fell in love with the opportunity, they fell in love with the process. Azariah and nine other teenagers had a dream. They dreamt of a better community. They dreamt of lasting change. They dreamt of fresh food, flowers, and community. Then they woke up for their dream and started putting it into action. Childlike faith.

It took a group of fifteen- and sixteen-year-old kids to change the community. Some didn't even have bank accounts. So we helped them set those up. Most of their summer employment opportunities had disappeared because of COVID-19; working at this open-air food mart turned out to be the perfect opportunity for these kids to do work that made a real difference.

Change starts with you. But it doesn't end there. It continues with a team. And our team was growing.

A TEAM BUILT ON TRUST

The By the Hand Club for Kids is an after-school program based out of Chicago. It was started about two decades ago by a woman named Donnita Travis, a marketing executive who left her role at a growing marketing firm after God gave her a dream of changing the city of Chicago. Trading her six-figure marketing job for a journey into the unknown, she went straight to the most avoided areas in Chicago and set up shop. She started with sixteen kids. Now her organization serves over sixteen hundred, walking with children who live in underresourced neighborhoods so they can have abundant lives.

By the Hand was one of five nonprofits my teammates and I had partnered with in 2018, a couple of years before the dream for the pop-up food mart began to form. We'd developed such a close connection and deep trust over those years that they were who I called when I wanted to sit with the kids in 2020 and figure out how we could best serve their community. Donnita provided an open door.

Trust is essential for change. I trust Donnita with my time, my relationships, and my resources. And she trusts me. But I'm not the only one she trusts. Ricardo (name changed) is an ex-con. He was involved in gang activity as a teenager, and because of that he'd spent twenty-four years in prison. During that time he had an encounter with Jesus, and that encounter changed his life forever. Upon his release, Donnita offered Ricardo a job. It was a low-paying security job, but he took it seriously.

One Friday afternoon Donnita was expecting a check. She didn't know when it would come and had a prior commitment. So she asked if Ricardo would wait at the facility and receive the package. He did. He waited and waited but no one came. No package was delivered. Then he had an idea. Some would call it an intuition, others would call it the Holy Spirit. Whatever the source of inspiration, he decided to go check a different address. He wondered if the sender had made a mistake and scrambled the directional in the street address. He walked a mile down the street from North Laramie to South Laramie, rang the doorbell, and asked if they had received a package. Sure enough, they had. He was elated and called Donnita to ask what he should do. She thought and thought. After what seemed like an eternity, she said, "Hold on to it. I'll come and get it tomorrow."

Now, you need to know what this important package was. It was a million-dollar check. Ricardo later described that moment as the most meaningful of his life. This ex-con, this man who had been cast off by society, had been lifted up by one person who made a simple decision. Donnita chose to trust Ricardo. And Ricardo's life would never be the same. Ricardo now holds the keys to a multimillion-dollar facility. He helps run the nonprofit.

We raised the money, By the Hand facilitated meetings, and the kids ran the food mart. I love showing up and providing inspirational leadership, but I left the planning to the professionals. Donnita and her team organized meetings with architects and other planners. The young entrepreneurs did all the designs and chose the name—and most important, they showed up and did the work. They ran the facility for months.

We knew a pop-up mart wasn't a sustainable, long-term solution. But when the kids showed they were committed, the community was inspired and it opened the door for a more permanent answer to the West Side food desert.

The next year we hosted a twenty-four-hour radiothon

When you have the
courage to follow the
fire, you are providing
a light for others to
see, inspiring and
empowering them to
discover and follow
their own fires.

in partnership with a local Chicago radio station, and we raised enough funds to help build a permanent facility. Today that facility is up and running, with a few new entrepreneurs at the helm. I couldn't be happier.

When you follow your fire, it's contagious. Your fire is *meant* to be caught by others. When you have the courage to follow the fire, you are providing a light for others to see, inspiring and empowering them to discover and follow their own fires. And once it gets caught, it's unstoppable.

Be bold enough to be the spark. Provide the light. And see how following the fire can turn you into a change-maker.

FOUR

FUEL YOUR FIRE

C hange is hard. There will be occasions when you become discouraged. During times like these, all you need is a word to encourage you. All you need is a spark to get the fire going again. As I was in the process of writing this book, I went to Nigeria for my grandmother's funeral and I got two of those sparks.

The first spark I got was an email from my former publicist. She told me about her nephew, who had gotten into some trouble at school and was feeling really down. He wasn't the one who caused the issue, but he was the president of his class, so when the class got punished, he got punished too. He had to repeat a grade and he was feeling discouraged. She went on to tell me that her nephew had read my book *Let the World See You* and it helped him get out of his slump. The subject line of her email was "Random in-real-life story," and random it was. But she found out how much my book had helped her nephew, so she decided to share the story with me.

Soon thereafter I received another email from a woman who had just started working with the Wuerffel Foundation, which exists to inspire greater service and unity in our communities. I had won the Wuerffel Trophy in college and this woman was inviting me to a reunion. But in addition to the invite, she gave me an ounce of encouragement. At the very end of her email invitation she added this postscript: "We so enjoy seeing your smile on ESPN; you make the world a brighter place!"

Neither of these women knew what I was going through, or that I was attending the funeral of a woman my family loved, or how discouraged I was in the writing process. But they were adding fuel to my fire. They were providing hope in the midst of my discouragement. They were fanning the flames.

Upon returning to the States, I received another text message from a friend. This friend is a *New York Times* bestselling author and a huge college football fan. Her team was playing in the national championship game and I happened to be getting ready to watch. She asked how my family and I were doing after the funeral, and I started to type a response. The words that flowed out of my fingers were probably more than the norm for a text message, but I was encouraging her and myself. We were talking about sports, but we were also talking about life. We talked about faith and disappointment, courage and hope. It was intense. I nearly apologized. I was certain this wasn't what she wanted to hear just minutes before her team played such a huge game. But her response nearly brought me to tears.

What you wrote is so beautiful, she said. And I loved reading it. This successful author, who is a leader and role model for many, affirmed me. She added oxygen to the flames that had been sparked by those previous emails.

LIGHT TO SHOW THE WAY

The only way to maneuver in darkness is with light. When I was in Nigeria at my grandma's house, and the lights would turn off and the atmosphere was pitch black, our answer to the darkness was a small, light-weight, kerosene lamp. If you needed to go anywhere in the village at nighttime, a lantern was your best chance. You would strike a match to light the wick, and the burning wick would provide sustained light in the dark night. The way a wick works is by consuming the oil hidden in the base of the lantern. The wick pulls up the oil using capillary action, and that oil sustains the fire. Wicks work against gravity, continually drawing the oil up and providing fuel to the fire. But it's not just oil that sustains these fires. The fire from kerosene lamps needs oxygen too; all fires do.

Surround yourself
with people who
believe in you.
People who
challenge you to be
your best, who trust
you with million-
dollar checks.

Kerosene and oxygen. Fire needs both a fuel source and the right environment—and it's the same for you and me. Surround yourself with people who believe in you. People who challenge you to be your best, who trust you with million-dollar checks.

Don't misunderstand me here. I'm *not* saying you should surround yourself only with people who automatically affirm everything you say and do. That's not genuine fuel for your fire. Sometimes you need to hear hard truths. A friend of mine recently did this for me. His words were simultaneously tough to hear and incredibly encouraging—a criticism followed by an affirmation. "Sam," he said, "you discount yourself and your abilities. If you ever started believing in yourself, in your abilities, the whole world would change."

One thing I remember about those village nights with the lantern is that the wicks needed to be trimmed between each use. After the wick provided light, the charred part needed to be removed. If it isn't trimmed after each use, a wick is ineffective because the burnt edges won't catch fire.

I didn't see what my friend did. He saw the wick and he saw the char. He knew about the times that I'd been burnt before. He knew that I hadn't addressed those times. He saw the pain that I had chosen to ignore. He saw me. And ever so kindly and graciously, he spoke the truth. He gave me oxygen and added fuel to my fire. He helped me address the burnt edges, the chars, the scars.

We've all been scared and scarred, hurt and in need of help.

We've been beaten and berated.

Yes, we've all experienced pain. But many of us haven't addressed it. We know we need healing and help, but we choose against it, afraid of what it might cost us. We're afraid of assessing and addressing the damage, so we sit there, broken. It's no surprise then when the things that used to light us up no longer bring us joy. That the person we used to be no longer has a spark.

We're charred.

But the great thing about fire is that all it takes to get it burning again is oxygen, fuel, and a little bit of trimming. Find those people who fuel you. Who provide you with the oxygen you need to burn bright. Who aren't afraid to trim your charred edges so you can light up the world once again.

WATCH OUT FOR FIRE QUENCHERS

Receiving encouragement, pursuing healing, and surrounding yourself with a community are ways of adding fuel to your fire. But there are also things that can choke your fire out if you're not careful. I've discovered a few things over the years that make the fire sputter and smoke and start to die down. I'm hoping my story can help you avoid those fire quenchers in your own life.

Fire Quencher #1: Doubting Your Value

Recently I bought a new car. It was a luxury vehicle that I had been dreaming about owning. I'm not a car guy. But this experience was less about buying a new car and more about showing the world that I'm a man. I was making a big decision and I was ready to declare this truth.

But first, a little background. When I graduated from college and got drafted in the NFL, I used my signing bonus to buy a brand-new 2011 Range Rover Sport. That thing was sweet. Black on black with twenty-two-inch rims with red trim. This car had a special edition Kahn Kit on it, which was a uniquely designed kit molded to the car as it was being made. I loved it.

Although I paid for the car, I didn't pick it out. My dad did. He was living in Dallas and had a great relationship with the owner of the Range Rover dealership. My dad isn't in the car business, but he loves nice cars. When he saw the car, he knew it was for me. He and the dealer showed me pictures and I was sold. I trusted my dad. He had never led me wrong. And it turned out to be one of the best decisions I've ever made.

After I drove it off the lot, it seemed as if at every red light a different driver or passerby was looking at my wheels, trim, or accents with awe. I even got a few honks of admiration from other vehicles. But even though this vehicle was undeniably amazing, I started taking it for granted. Instead of being grateful, I became self-conscious that the decision had been made for me. Even so, when I got into a wreck about eight years later, I was devastated.

I remember my dad telling me there was no other car like it in the world, but at the time I didn't know if that was hyperbole or truth. Turns out, it was no exaggeration. After the wreck I spent months looking for new parts. There were none to be found—not in America, not in London, nowhere. The car had been molded, welded together, with the exact pieces made for that specific car. It was truly one of a kind. And now it was gone.

We do that to ourselves sometimes: forget—or doubt—our value. We forget that there's no one like us in the whole world and that we can't be replaced. We forget that God almighty, the God who created the heavens and the earth, also created you and me with specific gifts and purposes. Or maybe we heard this a long time ago and believed it then, but we fail to believe it now, thinking that whoever told us about our special uniqueness was exaggerating. That we couldn't be *that* special.

But I'm here to tell you that it is no embellishment or exaggeration when I say you are uniquely irreplaceable. You are more valuable than any vehicle. You are God's best gift. His best creation. And even if you wreck what was a one-of-a-kind model, God can restore you. That's what he does. He's a healer, a redeemer.

Fire Quencher #2: Getting Distracted

After my failure to find replacement parts after the wreck, it became clear that I needed a new vehicle. And this time I was determined to make my own decision and pick out my next car myself.

It had to be big. It had to be new. It had to stand out. I set my eyes on an Infiniti QX80 Limited Edition. I had to have it. For a guy who's not into cars, I found myself falling in love with this vehicle. I did my research and studied different aspects of the car, looking at kits, comps, add-ons, and adjustments. I couldn't wait for it to come out, and when the new model arrived at the dealership, I was the first person there.

Sometimes we get trapped by lies and lusts, by fears and feelings of insecurity. There's something inside of us believing we're not enough. When we doubt our value, more often than not we start feeling pulled toward dis-tractions, toward idols. And this leads us to make bad or uninformed decisions. No matter how much the pur-chase costs, how right the relationship seems, or how perfect the person appears to be, they will never satisfy.

As soon as I purchased my new Infiniti, I felt duped. I felt I had been tricked into purchasing add-ons that I had no interest in, and I was left waiting for hours while finance was working on paperwork. I had arrived midafternoon, but I had to leave to go speak at an event that evening.

"You don't have to pay now," they told me. "Feel free to take the car and come back tomorrow."

Something seems odd about this, I thought as I drove off the lot in my new car. I hadn't paid, but I had already signed the paperwork. I went back the next day to pay and finish up. But in that twenty-four-hour period, the regret I felt outweighed my joy in the new purchase. So I asked if I could cancel some of the extras that I didn't want.

"Eh," the man began, "I'm not so sure that's can-cellable. I'll have to double-check."

I was so angry. I knew this double-checking would add even more time to this lengthy process, and I was ready to be done with the ordeal. I waited and waited and still didn't hear an answer. So I paid my money and

Sometimes pain

is the perfect

teacher. Losses

can be life's

greatest lessons.

left, feeling sick. To add insult to injury, my dad had been there the day before. He had been willing to help me navigate the process of buying a new vehicle, but I'd brushed him off. I wanted this to be *my* moment. But it didn't turn out how I'd hoped.

Fire Quencher #3: Giving In to Shame and Regret

Sometimes pain is the perfect teacher. Losses can be life's greatest lessons. I was so hurt, frustrated, and disappointed in myself. I didn't want to go back home. I felt ashamed.

The next few days were tough for me. Driving—or even walking past—the car brought up feelings of regret. My shining moment had backfired. And then one day I was coming back from work and decided to slow down before pulling into my garage. I stopped and parked in the driveway. As I was sitting there, I saw a stack of white papers sticking out of the glove compartment. They were the hard copies of the electronic paperwork I had signed just a few days earlier. I hadn't read them, but I noticed them now and decided to check them out.

Below every single one of these additions that I hadn't wanted, I saw in small, fine print that they were indeed cancellable within twenty-five days—and some even forty-five days. It had been five days.

That's the thing about idols. When we make the

mistake of thinking we can be satisfied or fulfilled by an idol, we eventually start to feel stuck, trapped by the very thing we'd been pursuing. But we're not. Always remember: You are never trapped. You never have to settle for something or someone that isn't right for you. You always have a choice. You just have to read the fine print.

I decided to keep the car and cancel all of the add-ons. But after all that, I *still* did not enjoy that car! And looking back, I could see the path that had brought me there. My insecurity and undervaluing myself led directly to my obsession with picking out the perfect vehicle, as if the act of discovering and acquiring it would bring me happiness and fulfilment. I got distracted from what really matters. I made a bad choice. And now I was dealing with regret and shame.

It might seem like I'm reading a lot into this situation—after all, I was just buying a new vehicle! But I'm telling you, I approached this in a way that quenched my fire. Giving in to insecurity, getting distracted, and dealing with regrets is a cycle that you've got to avoid if you're going to follow the fire and pursue your dreams.

About a year later I traded in the car for a Range Rover at the same dealership where my dad had bought my first one a decade before. When I walked in the dealer recognized me. "Sam!" he greeted me. After some small talk, he said, "You know, I'm still sad about that car."

I wasn't sure what he was talking about, so I asked, "You mean the one from 2011?"

"Yeah, man," he responded. "That thing was truly one of a kind." My dad was right. No exaggeration, no pretending. It was one of one.

So are you. God wants to grow you to embrace your one-of-a-kind identity and purpose. The world will try to sell you an identity or a purpose that'll leave you feeling empty—and it'll use your pain and your fears to do it. Let Jesus see your pain, your scars, your fears and regret. And believe him when he says that you are his. I traded in my pain, and God replaced it with a new and improved me. I have been redeemed.

I still drive that Range Rover. And when I look at it, there are no feelings of shame or remorse—all I feel is grateful. Grateful that I had been there, lost myself, and come back again.

We all have moments when we've been burned and feel like giving up. When we've gotten into that cycle of insecurity, distraction, and regrets. We feel like all our attempts to find healing and wholeness have failed, so why try again? Maybe we even start to feel jaded. Well, I'm here to tell you that there is a way out. Maybe you need to open your glove compartment and read the fine print. Maybe you need to address the issue that you've ignored for so long. But even when your fire has been quenched, there are opportunities to refuel and reignite.

Learn to embrace the things that fuel your fire and learn to avoid the fire quenchers. These words are just as much for me as they are for you. I can't write about something I'm not committed to living out. I'm committing to taking the journey with you. This is not a "how to" book. It's a "let's do" book. So let's keep each other encouraged. The better we get at adding fuel to each other's fires (and guarding against the fire quenchers), the more effective we'll be as real changemakers.

FIVE

YOUR DREAM
IS NOT JUST
FOR YOU

As I was reading the story of Nehemiah, the name Azariah kept popping up. Azariah is a Hebrew name that means "helped by God."[1] There are a few Azariahs in the Bible. The Azariah in this story was one of the men with Nehemiah in Jerusalem helping to rebuild the wall.[2]

As you'll remember, Azariah is also the name of the teenage girl who was on the bus the day we toured the West Side, the one whose comments fueled us. We left that bus ride with Azariah determined to make a change. As a matter of fact, my story would not be complete without Azariah. Just like her namesake, she showed up and the fire grew. Sometimes you need other people to help fuel your fire and write your story. And sometimes you need to help them with theirs.

Nehemiah couldn't rebuild Jerusalem's wall by himself, so he fanned the flame to encourage others to join his journey, including Azariah.[3] When you fuel your story and fan the flames, you give others an opportunity to believe. They may even encourage you.

Hearing the teenage Azariah's story fanned my flame. Seeing her brilliance and her resilience, her focus and her fight, encouraged me to say yes, to show up, to put my hands to good work. Sometimes all you need is an encouraging word. Other times, you just need to see the example of another.

I was sitting in a library working on this book when a situation outside caught my eye. There was an older man on the street who'd stopped on his way from the grocery store to his car. He bent down at the edge of the sidewalk as if he had dropped something, but then I realized he wasn't stooping to pick anything up. He was stuck. His knees were shaking. I was starting to wonder whether I should go offer help when a car stopped and a young man jumped out. Instead of driving by and ignoring the older man, he parked his car in the middle of the street and helped a stranger to his destination.

After making sure the old man was okay, this modern-day Good Samaritan raced back to his car—a long line of vehicles had already started to form behind him—and continued on his way. That experience still hasn't left me. It never will. The humanity of this small act of kindness reminded me of what I'm trying to build. Heaven on earth. A place where human flourishing can exist without fear or pretense, without pride or falsehood. That young man was providing a light for me that he may never even know about.

Following the fire is not just for you. It's for countless

Following the fire
is not just for you.
It's for countless
others you may
never meet.

others you may never meet. You never know who may be watching or how even a small act of kindness might have a ripple effect.

ONE CHANGE LEADS TO TRANSFORMATION

I shared with you in the last chapter about Donnita Travis, founder and executive director of By the Hand, an after-school program that creates places where kids can come and get holistic mentoring and community. She wanted to go where the people were hurting the most, so she chose locations with the most gang activity, the most violence, the most destruction. And the building they chose as their headquarters was emblematic of the transformation they were aiming for. The location was a former nightclub that was known for violence, prostitution, and gang activity. But after By the Hand purchased it, it became a beacon of hope.

Donnita was on to something. Buildings provide a symbol that people can hold on to even when belief is hard to come by. Nehemiah knew this and so did Donnita. The By the Hand Club in the Austin neighborhood provided hope. According to Azariah, it made her community feel a lot homier. Think about that for a minute. A single building can change an entire neighborhood. It can make an entire community feel more like a home.

So when we saw the liquor store next door to the kid's club, we saw the potential. The kids had to walk by it every single day on their way to and from their after-school program. The violence was palpable. The danger was real. But I couldn't get that idea out of my head that one change can transform an entire community. *Well,* I thought, *if the former club was the living room, a former liquor store would make a pretty good kitchen.*

One thing I hadn't realized in my pursuit is that many members of the community had been trying to get rid of that liquor store for over twenty years. People had been praying for that community to change for two decades. But business was booming. The store had no reason to sell. Until COVID hit.

Jon, a fortysomething white dude from the suburbs, had been praying for that community for years. He wanted to see change, but he didn't know what to do. So every Friday night from six until about midnight, he walked the streets of Austin and prayed. When he heard about our purchase of the liquor store, he reached out through a friend to say thank you.

You may never know who's watching or whose prayers you're answering.

I had seen what investing in a community can do. Ever since I was fifteen years old, I've been going on medical mission trips with my family. I've seen my dad build houses and hospitals, and I've seen the difference these buildings can bring. The fire in my father's heart was starting to catch in my own heart. His compound and the hospital brought hope to a hopeless situation in our village in Nigeria. The healthy food store was about to do the same in Chicago.

Purchasing this liquor store made perfect sense as a next step. Not only would we be adding an oasis to this food desert, but we would also be decreasing the gang activity. I asked Azariah what she wanted the new food store to look like. She started dreaming, and we started counting the cost.

IGNORE THE DOUBTERS

Azariah continued showing up. As did I. Together we were able to light up a city. And that light cannot be denied.

Fire has a unique smell. It also provides warmth for your body and light for your eyes to see. If you're close enough, you can even hear it. There's no doubt that when Nehemiah and his friends were rebuilding the wall in Jerusalem, people in surrounding areas knew about it. "Now it came about that when Sanballat heard that we were rebuilding the wall, he became furious and very angry, and he mocked the Jews."[4]

People won't always be happy when they see you following your fire. Ignore them. Detractors may despise your good works. Doubters will undoubtedly arise. They will try to rain on your parade. They will try to put out your fire. Get used to them, but don't listen to them. Instead, do like Nehemiah did: keep on working. That's been Azariah's response. She could have listened to her doubters. The classmates who mocked her moxie, the people who doubted her destiny. But she didn't. Instead, she did the opposite. She grew louder, she stepped up, and she kept working.

Here's a story that may be familiar to you. In the book of Daniel we read about a man who was thrown into a lions' den and came out unscathed. But Daniel had some friends who did something just as brave. They were thrown into a fire and came out fine. His friends were Hananiah, Mishael, and, you guessed it, Azariah.

After King Nebuchadnezzar of Babylon conquered Jerusalem, he wanted to bring back young, good-looking, intelligent people from the region to work for him. Daniel, Hananiah, Mishael, and Azariah were among those selected to serve at court. Sometime later, the king had a golden idol built and commanded that everyone bow down to it. Whoever refused would be thrown into a furnace of blazing fire.[5] Azariah, Mishael, and Hananiah, who by this time were managing a province in Babylon, got caught refusing to worship the statue.

When you're standing up for something you believe in, things will get hot. Things will not be easy. You will face doubt and resistance. You may be treated like trash. You might even have your very life threatened.

When Azariah and his two friends refused to bow down, they were told to either give up their beliefs or die.[6] There will come a time when your beliefs, what you choose to stand for, will be tested. You must decide beforehand how you will respond.

My friend Cindy is a seventy-year-old white woman who lives in Houston and grew up in Amarillo. She has tried to educate herself about racism and address inequalities, but many of her friends haven't. Once, while sitting at her favorite restaurant, her friend noticed a few Black people dining there.

"There are so many of them here," her friend said. "I hope you're happy."

Cindy was shocked that her friend could be so callous toward people who were made in the image of God.

"Don't say that," Cindy responded to her friend.

YOUR DREAM IS NOT JUST FOR YOU

"These people are no different than you and me. And we need to love them accordingly."

Cindy faced the fire that day. She lost a friend in the process. But she came out better than before. Prepare to face the fire. Decide beforehand how you'll react when you're tested.

Azariah and his friends refused to worship anything besides God. No compromise. But after being tied up and thrown into the blazing furnace, they came out untouched by the fire.[7] Not a hair on their heads had been singed, not a thread of their clothing had been burned. The result of their bravery? King Nebuchadnezzar changed his decree and gave the Hebrew people the freedom to worship God. Think about it—this was the most powerful nation in the world at the time, with oppressive policies against religious freedom and a willingness to use extreme violence against its own citizens to enforce those policies. But the brave actions of just three young people created powerful change at the highest levels and brought freedom and justice for an entire community.

That's what I mean when I say your dream isn't just for you. The things you care about in your heart are going to lead you to action. That's faith. And your faithful actions just might bring large-scale change.

What lengths would you be willing to go to if you knew you could bring positive change for your community? For your family? For yourself? The world needs you. It's time.

GET COMFORTABLE WITH FEELING UNCOMFORTABLE

If you're stepping out in faith, you're going to feel uncomfortable sometimes. Speaking up about injustice invites scrutiny. Getting close enough to the suffering of others to make a difference in their lives will sometimes break your heart. But if your dream isn't just for you—if it's going to grow into a changemaking force that impacts the lives of others—you're going to have to get comfortable with feeling uncomfortable.

For years I've helped lead an annual medical mission trip to Nigeria. But recently I felt the Spirit of God telling me to say no and stay available for a different opportunity. I was ready for something new. And sure enough, shortly after I canceled my Nigeria plans, an opportunity with IJM (International Justice Mission) in Guatemala arose.

I'm going to share more details about IJM a little later. But for now, I'll just say that IJM is a global organization that combats slavery, violence against women and children, and abuse of power against people who are poor.[8] I had heard about this organization, but I had never had a chance to look closely at their work. Long story short, I got involved with IJM as an ambassador, someone who uses their influence to advocate for IJM's work. And as part of my role, I had the privilege of taking a short but incredibly impactful three-day trip to Guatemala.

While in Guatemala with IJM, I met kids who had experienced the worst kinds of abuse. Children who had been enslaved, abused, and exploited. These words are difficult to write. Evil is real. It's very real. But so is good; so is love. And love overcomes evil. I cried real tears in Guatemala. But I felt strong too.

While there, I was able to use my gifts for justice. I had taken Spanish in high school and in college. And though I wasn't fluent, when I spent those days in Guatemala, my Spanish started to come back. I began to pray, to write, and even to speak publicly in Spanish. I spoke to men about ways they could step up and lead. I wasn't fluent, but I was able to use gifts that had been dormant for years.

My NFL career opened up doors too. Since I played in the NFL, people in this foreign country were willing to listen to me. I went to radio stations and spoke to

We love to avoid the mess, thinking that beauty comes naturally. But if I think back on my life, I see that time and time again the most beautiful moments stemmed from the hardest seasons.

people about what IJM was doing to help and how they could join the effort. I told people about why we came and the work that the people in the local field office were doing to create change. Getting uncomfortable brought out the best in me.

What gifts are asleep in you? What desires have you neglected? Pressure makes diamonds. Beauty lies beneath the mess. We love to avoid the mess, thinking that beauty comes naturally. But if I think back on my life, I see that time and time again the most beautiful moments stemmed from the hardest seasons.

We're taught to fear the things we don't know. To be suspicious of people who look, act, or think differently than us. We're taught that following fear is the safest way to live. But I'm learning that the opposite is true. I'm learning that the only way to truly live is to lean into the things that stretch me beyond my comfort zone. Are you willing to stretch beyond yours?

SIX

BE CURIOUS.
STAY OPEN.

Creating change requires knowledge and a willingness to do something with that knowledge. You have to know an issue exists before you can address it. And once you know, you have to be willing to go. If you want to be a changemaker, you're going to need to foster two important qualities: curiosity and openness. Asking questions can lead not only to a clearer understanding of a problem but also to better answers and stronger solutions. And when those answers and solutions become clear, don't close yourself off. Instead, open yourself up to how you can get involved.

WHEN SOMETHING DOESN'T FEEL RIGHT

It's interesting the things we take for granted: light, electricity, running water. Things that are so common to many of us but so rare for others. And when I say *others*, I don't just mean people in developing countries. Some people in the same cities as us—the same zip codes and even right around the corner—lack these essentials.

While driving through the West Side of Chicago a few years back I was arrested—not by a member of law enforcement but by my emotions. After riding through one of the nicest parts of town, I was shocked to turn a corner and see a different reality. The view went from beautiful homes to abandoned buildings, bustling streets to a ghost town. From parks and playgrounds to dirt and dust. On one side, most people's idea of America. On another, a developing country. It looked like some of the villages I'd visited in Nigeria. The only division between the two sides was the train tracks.

As we passed more homes, I thought, *This place is beautiful.* A minute later I was astounded again by the decay on the other side of the street. I asked the driver if he knew much about this side of town.

"How much do these homes cost?" I asked.

"These are Greystones," he explained. "Some of the most beautiful homes in town. You could probably buy any one of these homes for sixty to a hundred thousand dollars." I was shocked—and ready to take some money out of my savings account and put it into a home or two! But before I could finish my thought we came to a red light, and he continued talking. "You wouldn't wanna live here though. This corner had over thirty shootings last weekend. Ten people died here just a few days ago."

I was speechless. How could this beautiful corner contain so much death, so much violence? I was also confused as to why the homes were so cheap. My driver went on to tell me how the property taxes had been raised to the point that the current homeowners, nearly all African American people, could no longer afford to live there. They were moving out in droves. And investors were already purchasing their properties. In ten to fifteen years, these would be million-dollar homes.

Something about that process didn't feel right. These homeowners were trying to build families, wealth, and stability to make things better for future generations. And out of nowhere, the tax rate skyrocketed. I didn't know what to do.

Part of me wanted to buy a few houses to keep the investors from getting their hands on them. I wanted these homeowners to live there without fear of being kicked out. I knew something had to be done. When the light turned green, we continued on our journey. I peppered this man with more questions. He provided some answers and recommended resources such as *The Color of Law* by Richard Rothstein and *Divided by Faith* by Michael O. Emerson. I went on to research and found this in a publication about Chicago Greystones and their importance:

> Neighborhoods are fundamentally about the dynamic relationship between people, buildings and a given place. Families move in and move out; buildings get fixed; new homes are built; businesses open and close; and the people who live in the neighborhoods get involved in block clubs and community groups, get to know their neighbors, raise their children, and put down their own roots. Across Chicago, Greystone homes have played an important role in this process for more than 100 years.[1]

That's why it was so devastating when these homes—homes that were constructed as a bridge for lower-income families to build toward the middle class—were having taxes raised seemingly overnight to force the predominantly Black tenants out.

Once I made it to the school where I was scheduled to speak, I asked more questions while talking with some of the faculty. I wanted to better understand their reality. Two hours passed and the driver was waiting, so I reluctantly left the school with more questions than answers. But I'd found something that was wrong, and I was ready to start digging deeper.

There's a way to channel our anger, our frustration, our passion, and take aim. Harness those emotions and focus on addressing the problem. I'm learning the power of naming my emotions.

Have you ever had this feeling that something wasn't right? Something wasn't fair, but you couldn't exactly put your finger on it? You might feel helplessness overtake you. I've felt the same way. But we don't have to stop at the feeling. There's a way to channel our anger, our frustration, our passion, and take aim. Harness those emotions and focus on addressing the problem. I'm learning the power of naming my emotions. But beyond that, we can use these emotions to create rather than destroy. To build up rather than break down. To encourage rather than wallow. I'm learning how to be an agent of change. I'm learning how to lead.

You *can* see injustice and address it. You *can* stand in the gap for those who are hurting. You *can* use what you have: your eyes, hands, feet, and heart to make a change. You *can* stand up for justice. You *can* lead in your community, family, school, and suburb. Leaders come in different shapes and sizes, with unique gifts, talents, and abilities. But leadership always comes back to the same basic reality: it's using what you have for the benefit of others. Nothing more, nothing less.

Don't just follow the fire; bring it with you. Bring your energy. Bring your kindness. Bring your passion. Be a light. People will see it and be changed. Following the fire is about what's on the inside. Find your fire and watch how far it will take you.

I still haven't figured out what to do with those Greystones, but I've got a feeling someone will. Maybe that person will be you.

LISTEN FOR THE SPIRIT'S VOICE

During the months leading up to the pandemic, we were living in Chicago. Everything was perfect where we were. The kids had a great school, my wife had a great community, our family had a great church, and I even had a place to work out. However, the Spirit of God was telling me to leave. And I didn't know how to explain it, but I was feeling a nudge to leave Chicago and go to Arizona. I was a bit confused, but I had learned over the years to listen to that voice and follow it. That's an important part of following the fire—paying attention when the Spirit is moving quietly but insistently in your heart. Don't ignore that voice. The sooner you listen, the better off you'll be.

I was due in Miami for an NFL Players Association meeting in early March 2020 and was planning to take the family. And my wife's appointment for her US citizenship, which we had waited five years for, was right around the corner.

"How about we wait until we get back from the

Miami trip to figure out our move to Arizona," my wife suggested. It made sense. But the voice of the Holy Spirit was so clear. *Go to Miami for the conference and don't come back. Go straight to Arizona.* I know that God often protects us from things that we may not even know about. He'll warn you if you listen. His Spirit will lead you and guide you. But unfortunately, I wasn't ready to listen. It felt too complicated and rushed to deal with all the details of moving to a new state before the Miami trip—so I didn't.

We left for Miami on March 9 and stayed beyond the conference to celebrate our anniversary. We planned to return to Chicago in time for my wife's citizenship appointment on March 22—staying in a hotel since a new tenant would already have moved into the house we'd been renting—and figure out the details. But while we were in Miami, COVID hit. School was canceled, church was closed, and the city of Chicago was shut down. Stay-at-home orders and a curfew had been issued for the entire city. We came back to the cold (yes, March in Chicago is *cold*), and were staying in a small hotel. Nothing was open. The citizenship appointment, which had been on the books since long before the pandemic, had been "de-scheduled" due to concerns about COVID. It was time to go—and I so wished I'd gone straight to Arizona from Miami!

I'd never seen an airport that empty. We breezed through security and sat down to wait at our gate. There was an older couple sitting behind us who got up and left as soon as we arrived. I didn't blame them. This early in the pandemic, fears were running high. We boarded the plane and began our journey to Arizona. I felt like we were back on track—the only issue was we still didn't know where we were going to stay. And I found myself wishing again that I'd listened to the Holy Spirit's leading and found a place in Arizona sooner.

We couldn't stay with friends, since at that point nobody knew what the deal was with COVID. We ended up staying at an Airbnb—but not even the one we initially chose. The Airbnb owner picked for us. He found out that we had three kids and assured us he had a property that would be much more convenient for a family. Initially, I wasn't so sure. I wanted to stay where I wanted to stay! But ultimately, we had to go with what was available.

I share all this to say that sometimes we need to let go. We need to let God do what God wants to do. The more I'd sidestepped the Spirit's voice or tried to hold on to my own plans, the worse our situation got. But when I was forced to let go, things started to work out.

Arizona proved to be the perfect place for us. There were fewer restrictions and the weather was much warmer. The place the Airbnb owner chose turned out to be just right. Plus it was next to an empty lot, so I had space to run, train, and prepare for the next football season. We grew as a family too. In-person church meetings were still canceled, so we chose church at home. We dressed up, got ready, got in our car, drove around the block, and walked back inside. We needed things to seem as normal as possible. We rearranged the living room so it felt different than usual. We sang, we prayed, we read the Bible, and we even gave our testimonies.

That time in Arizona was exactly what our family needed. We rested and refocused, bonded with each other, and enjoyed the warm weather. But after just two months, the Spirit of God was telling me it was time to go again. I was, however, torn about the next step. I had friends, family, and a place to stay in Texas, but I felt this tug to go back to Chicago. The place where we still had no place to stay. We had packed up our car and prepared to take a multi-day road trip. I told my wife and kids that we were going to Dallas. But I still wasn't convinced.

I didn't want to leave. And I definitely didn't want to go back to Texas. It didn't feel right. In order to buy time, I woke up early and swung by a friend's house to get a quick workout in. This was another case of me listening to God's voice. Usually I would have left first thing in the morning so that I could knock out as much of the drive as possible in day one. But I didn't. I waited for God's direction. Little did I know, he would be providing some guidance right on time.

As I was on my way to my friend's house, I stopped at a red light and checked my phone. An email notification popped up. It was from the United States Citizenship and Immigration Services, informing me that my wife's appointment, the one that had been de-scheduled, had now been rescheduled. It was going to take place in two weeks, back in Chicago. Confirmation. We were going back to Chicago.

Upon arriving we found a hotel and prepared for the appointment. Little did I know that God had brought me back to Chicago just in time to make some important connections. It was during our time in that hotel that I listened to the kids and got the athletes together, took that bus ride with Jason, and made the connection with Roger Goodell. It was when everything happened that got the wheels turning for the pop-up food mart and eventually the permanent Austin Harvest food store.

The point of this story is simple. Be curious. Stay open. Hold your own plans loosely, and always be ready to hear the voice, wisdom, and direction of God. If you've started fostering an attitude of openness and

If you've started fostering
an attitude of openness
and curiosity, a heart that's
sensitive to the guidance of
the Spirit and the suffering
of others, you'll be amazed
at how quickly God can
use you to create change.

curiosity, a heart that's sensitive to the guidance of the Spirit and the suffering of others, you'll be amazed at how quickly God can use you to create change. Staying open will bring you into unexpected seasons of blessing, and it'll open doors you weren't even looking for.

GOOD THINGS HAPPEN
WHEN YOU SAY YES

We are layered, deep, complex people and each one of us is unique; but at our core, I believe most of us share a hope to see this world become a better place. If you want to change your community, you must be willing to change yourself, your habits, and your life. That's what this book is about. Once you learn how to lead yourself, you'll have the opportunity to lead others. Build your own Austin Harvest. Write your own story. Make something beautiful. Sometimes all you need to do is say yes.

Say Yes Even When You're Not Sure
You Have What It Takes

I've met compulsive stutterers who now speak for a living. I've met people who were afraid to be on stage who now sing in front of thousands. People who were mute for half a decade are now using their voices to change lives. I'm a dude who hates cold weather but lives in Chicago! You never know how God will use you.

I had left Chicago in the past, but I felt the Lord asking me to return. If you've read *Let the World See You*, you'll remember that the house we were renting flooded at one point—and we were done with Chicago. We were ready to move on. But when I felt the Spirit of God telling me to go back, I said yes. Nearly a year after the flood, I decided to check online and see what was up with our old house. A little background: We loved that house. It was special to us. We'd rented it for four years and made multiple offers to buy it. Each offer was denied. Looking back, I can see that the timing wasn't right. But now the house was on the market! It had just been listed hours earlier, and it looked majestic. Brand-new paint on the walls, new flooring, new lights, even a new fridge. It seemed too good to be true. We bought it, and let me tell you, we are so glad to be home.

There are no accidents; everything happens for a reason. I would be remiss if I didn't tell you how this house story ends. Our home flooded because it couldn't withstand the extreme cold. We had a fireplace but hadn't used it in all the four years we'd lived there. In fact, I'd covered it up with the TV stand (forgive me y'all, I'm from Texas). And then, a polar vortex hit.

Temperatures sank to more than sixty degrees below zero, which caused the pipes to burst and the house to flood. Now that we were back, I was determined to figure out how to work the fireplace. We got rid of the TV stand that had been blocking it and mounted the TV in a different area. It still gets cold, but now we have a fire to keep us warm. I'm sitting just a few feet away from it as I write these words. Even though I hate the cold, Chicago has become my home. Saying yes to the Holy Spirit kept bringing me back here. I found life-giving purpose working with By the Hand and Austin Harvest, becoming a leader and changemaker. I found meaningful community. And now we finally own the home that we'd loved for years but hadn't been able to purchase despite many attempts to do so over the years.

Good things happen when you say yes.

Say Yes to Loving Your Neighbor

An expert in the law once came up to Jesus and asked, "Teacher, what shall I do to inherit eternal life?" Jesus confirmed what was written in the Law by saying, "You shall love the Lord your God with all your heart, and with all your soul, and with all your strength, and with all your mind; and your neighbor as yourself."[2] This man was an expert in the law, but not in love. How

115

many of us can relate? We know the rules, we know the laws, we know right from wrong, but we don't know how to love. We don't know how to sacrifice.

This man called Jesus by the name Teacher, but he had no true desire to learn. He wanted to be right. His heart was not in the right place. Have you ever been in a situation like this? I know I have. I've had times where I said all the right things, but in my heart I had no intention of changing. My main desire was to look good, to be right.

After Jesus explained the commandments, the man asked, "And who is my neighbor?"[3] I don't think the man really cared who his neighbor was. He wanted to look good and to justify himself. Jesus responded to the question with one of the most-repeated stories in history, the story of the Good Samaritan.

A man was going down from Jerusalem to Jericho and fell into the hands of robbers. They stripped him, beat him up, and fled, leaving him half dead. A priest happened to be going down that road. When he saw him, he passed by on the other side. In the same way, a Levite, when he arrived at the place and saw him, passed by on the other side. But a Samaritan on his journey came up to him, and when he saw the man, he had compassion. He went over to him and bandaged his wounds, pouring on olive oil and wine. Then he put him on his own animal, brought him to an inn, and took care of him. The next day he took out two denarii, gave them to the innkeeper, and said, "Take care of him. When I come back I'll reimburse you for whatever extra you spend."[4]

Jesus ended this story by asking the expert in the law which character in the story had proved to be a true neighbor to the man who had been robbed. The obvious answer is the Samaritan. But there's depth to the story. This expert was a religious man. He was a leader, an expert in the law. The two men who walked by in the story were also religious people, experts in the law, and important leaders. They were highly regarded in their communities. But both of them walked by and did nothing. Samaritans, on the other hand, were looked down on by the Jewish people of the time. But the Samaritan man who stopped to help used what he had and made a difference in the life of the man who'd been beaten and robbed. He sacrificed his time, talent, and treasure and became a model of love, a beacon of hope, an example for the world to see. This story reminds me that loving others has less to do with position and power and more to do with the posture of our hearts.

Nothing derails a potential changemaker faster than a tendency to say no when confronted with the unfamiliar, when faced with new opportunities, when given chances to love the people God has put in your path. You need to have a yes posture, an open heart, if you want to be a force for positive change.

Are you ready to say yes?

SEVEN

CHANGE ONLY HAPPENS THROUGH FOCUS

n football there's a simple saying: "Eyes take your hands; hands take your feet." What that means is that whichever direction you're looking is going to be the direction that your hands move when you go to strike someone or to make a tackle. And your feet will follow. If your eyes are focused on the wrong thing, you're done. You'll be out of position and give up a big play.

The same goes in life. If we're focused on the negative as opposed to the opportunities, we'll have no chance. The key word is *focused*. You can see the negative, but once you see it, address it and move on. Don't sulk in it. Don't sit in it. Change what you're looking at. Eyes take your hands.

If you want to be effective as a changemaker, you need to take some time to think about what you're focused on.

A WAKE-UP CALL

Recently my daughter was crying. Her tears came seemingly out of nowhere. I was working on a project, and I asked her to leave the room. She became even more distraught. I was surprised.

You can see the
negative, but once
you see it, address it
and move on. Don't
sulk in it. Don't sit
in it. Change what
you're looking at.
Eyes take your hands.

"Sophia, what's wrong?" I asked.

"I don't know, Daddy," she wailed.

I didn't believe her. "You can tell me, Sophia. What's wrong? Why are you crying?"

She responded as honestly as she knew how. Eyes full of tears, heart full of pain, she said, "Daddy, why are you always on the phone? Why do you always make so many calls and do so many meetings?"

I wished I had a good answer. Podcasts, Bible studies, business stuff—possible responses ran through my mind, but the fact of the matter is Sophia had noticed something. She noticed a dad who was always busy, distracted by many tasks. And now he was busy again. Her question still haunts me today, because it offers a healthy dose of truth.

It's been said that our kids spell *love* one way: T-I-M-E. My daughter was asking me, in her own way, "Daddy, do you love me? Will you sacrifice for me? Will you put me first?"

The answer is yes. The answer has to be yes.

Jesus spells *love* the same way. He doesn't want our busywork. He doesn't need our money or our possessions. He wants our time. He wants us. He created us for relationship with him and with others. He knows that when we serve others, we serve him. When we love others, we love him.

REMEMBER THE MAIN THING

Immediately after Jesus told the story of the Good Samaritan, there was another incident that speaks volumes about making time for God. Jesus entered a village and encountered two sisters, Mary and Martha. These sisters invited him to come into their home and rest. If you've heard enough stories from the life of Jesus in the Gospels, you'll know that these women interacted with Jesus often. They were close friends.

During this visit the Bible says that Martha was "distracted by her many tasks" while Mary sat at Jesus' feet.[1] I wonder how many of us want to make change in our lives, in our communities, in our families, but we're too distracted by our to-do lists and endless tasks to spend time with the people we should be caring for. We're preoccupied by things that we think matter but really don't. We think we're serving, helping, leading, and preparing—when in reality we're missing out on the main thing.

Going back to the story of the Good Samaritan, I wonder if the priest, when he saw the man who had been robbed, was distracted. Maybe he was too busy to stop. Maybe he had to go to the temple to pray. Maybe he had to get home after a long day's work. Maybe the Levite was busy too. Maybe he had an event that he needed to attend. He was just too busy. How many of us are too distracted or busy to love those around us? Too occupied to step into someone else's pain, to listen to their perspective? But love puts all else aside and chooses what's most important.

The Samaritan chose what was better, as did Mary. They chose to slow down, sacrifice, and serve. What are you willing to sacrifice to show those closest to you that you love them? Not just those who look like you, but those who don't. The poor, the hurting, the people on the other side of the train tracks.

We don't have to be like the priest or the Levite. We don't have to be like Martha either. We can be like Mary. We can be like the Samaritan. We can sit at Jesus' feet and listen to what he has to say. We can choose not to let ourselves be distracted and instead focus on helping others and spending time with the people who need our attention.

FOCUS ON FINDING
YOUR SUPERPOWER

Is there anything that you're naturally gifted at? Maybe it's a job or vocation, maybe it's a skill or a random talent. Some would call this a superpower. My superpower is with people. I want to see people and get to know them. One of my friends says I'm a relational ninja. I didn't understand what he meant until I met Poc.

In June of 2021 a friend and I went to a restaurant together. The restaurant was getting ready to close but we were still hungry. We asked the server if the chef wouldn't mind cooking up something extra even though the kitchen was closed. The chef obliged, and the food was phenomenal. I wanted to get to know the person who made it. So I asked the server if we could say thank you. A few moments later, Poc came walking out, introduced herself, and began to share her story.

Poc had been a sous chef for years, but life happened, so she moved to Austin and started working at this restaurant. Her smile lit up the restaurant, which we had noticed when we walked in. We complimented her on the meal and invited her to sit with us. And since the restaurant was closed, she did! We sat for a few minutes and learned about her life, her background, and her future aspirations. It was so cool. I felt so special. I think Poc did too. I want everyone to feel that way.

Finding your thing, then doing your thing. I didn't even realize that helping people feel special was my thing until my friend pointed it out to me.

"Sam," he said, "no one does that."

"Does what?" I asked, not sure what he was referring to.

"No one sits and talks to the chef and invites them to sit at their table just to hear their story."

I looked at him surprised, as if to say, "Why not?"

"That's your thing," he continued. "That's what makes you, you. Do that. Do more of that."

Sometimes you don't discover your thing—your fire—until someone points it out to you. But my friend's words rang true. Building a food mart, talking to a chef, and doing medical missions in Nigeria are all different on the outside. But on the inside they're driven by the same thing. They're all driven by my fire of wanting to build. Build people, build relationships, and sometimes, build buildings. My fire has to do with seeing others and allowing others to see me. To see their pain, to feel their struggle, and then to do something about it. Follow your fire. Your thing, however small it may seem, may turn into something bigger.

FOCUS ON THE PLACES WHERE PEOPLE ARE HURTING

The best leaders often come from broken backgrounds and painful pasts. And pain can be a powerful catalyst for change. After the pain of seeing Trayvon Martin killed in 2013, Ryan Wilson and his friend and former Georgetown roommate, T. K. Peterson, created a space where people can build, collaborate, and do business together. It's called The Gathering Spot.[2]

Initially it was going to be a talking club in Atlanta where Black people could come together and talk about social issues and racial justice, or simply spend time together and socialize. But then it became so much more. Atlanta is a city full of Black people, but they are often forgotten. So Ryan and T. K. built something they'd never had access to themselves.

At 12:42 a.m. on Sunday, July 14, hours after George Zimmerman was found not guilty for killing thirteen-year-old Trayvon Martin, Ryan sent a simple but strong text message to T. K. After expressing his anger and frustration, he simply said, I think it's time for us to step up. He went on to say in an interview years later,

I'll be honest with you. It's taken us a while for us to share this story. We always wanted to make sure that we were respectful to Trayvon and to his family. And part of us thought that no one would actually believe that this was the true start of The Gathering Spot; but this was it. TGS was born out of pain and out of frustration, and ultimately out of the belief that if we came together as a community that that was the only real way to move forward. My answer to the question, "What are we going to do?" was The Gathering Spot.[3]

When I first visited The Gathering Spot, it immediately felt like home. But interestingly, I showed up by accident. I had been to Atlanta a few times, usually for football-related activities. I attended Super Bowl festivities in the city and played games in its stadium. But this time I was in Atlanta to see a friend.

Tedashii Anderson is a musical artist. I met him at a concert and we eventually became close friends. During the pandemic we had started leading an online Bible study together and I decided to pay him a visit. Out of nowhere the Spirit of God was telling me to go to Atlanta. It was strange. There were about twelve of us in this Bible study group, but for whatever reason, God was telling me to go to Atlanta and visit Tedashii. He hadn't said anything, but somehow I knew Tedashii needed me. I knew he needed a hug. I needed one, too, and I wanted to be there for my friend.

So I booked my flight for the same night after our virtual Bible study. It was supposed to be a short trip—leave that night, come back the next. But since Bible study was so good, I ended up missing my flight. Rather than cancel the trip, I woke up early the next morning and hopped on another flight. I didn't know where we would meet until he suggested The Gathering Spot. So I put in the address, hopped into a rideshare, and commenced the long commute.

I didn't know what The Gathering Spot was at this point, but I knew why I was going there. This happens to me often. I'll commence a journey, not sure of the destination but completely certain of my purpose. I was there to be with my friend. Everything else was just icing on the cake. Thankfully, the cake was sweet. I showed up on a wet, rainy day. I wasn't paying much attention; I was just hoping I wouldn't be late. I arrived in front of what looked like a premium, exclusive gym. I would come to find that membership wasn't pricey; it was just based on intent. The goal was to have people there who needed community or a safe space. The place gave me hope.

Focus your attention where people are hurting, where they need help and community. If you put your focus there, chances are you'll see something you can do to make a difference.

FOCUS ON GRACE

I recently went to visit one of my friends. He had just lost someone close to him. He was distraught. He thought it was his fault. His eyes were full of tears when we were on the video call. I decided to hop on a plane. The Spirit of God kept on telling me to go. There was no doubt. I had just come back from my first speaking gig of the year, and I was excited to be home. Fall had been a busy season. Traveling five days a week, missing my wife and kids. I was ready to slow down and spend time at home. But after this call, after seeing my friend like this, it was an easy decision to go.

When I landed, I took an Uber and headed straight to him. He was not in good shape. He was full of shame. Full of regret. Full of fear, sadness, and remorse. I didn't know what to do, so I just sat. There was a game on, so we watched that. Little by little he started to open up. He started to let it out.

Quick aside: If you've ever done something that you think no one will forgive you for, or said something that you wish you could take back, or gone somewhere or thought something that you deeply regret—I've been there. We've all been there. You are loved. You are seen. You are forgiven. *Forgiveness* is a strong word, but it's the only appropriate word that properly explains where you stand in God's eyes. "If we confess our sins, He is faithful and righteous, so that He will forgive us our sins and cleanse us from all unrighteousness."[4] But the key is to confess. The secret is to say it. The Enemy wants you to keep it in. He wants you to be full of defeat. But Jesus wants to fill you with his forgiveness. Speak.

Little by little, day by day, my friend started opening up. He started talking more, he started sharing more of his feelings. By the time I was ready to go, he seemed to be in better shape than before—but I knew he still had a long way to go.

Sometimes, when we focus, we discover things that we didn't know were there. Much like the bus trip when we saw the food desert on the West Side of Chicago—we went for one thing, but we saw another.

As that week with my friend ended, I left encouraged. *Now I know what to pray for*, I thought. But I also saw something in myself. Something that needed to change. As much as I want to love people well, certain situations will bring anger out of my heart. Instead of blaming the other person for these situations, I'm learning to look within. For example, my oldest son was having trouble sleeping. And I was frustrated. I was angry because I wanted him to act like an adult, not a little kid. That sounds crazy to say because he's only seven years old, but it's true. Too often when he does something childish, I get angry. And I don't like that side of me. It's something I need to work on.

I saw and felt that anger when I went to visit my

Change starts with you—and sometimes it's you who needs to change before you can start bringing change to the world around you.

friend. He was lost, yes, but while I was spending time with him and sharing in his pain, something evil came out of me. So much so that I actually roared aloud. I was so angry. I was there to help my friend, but things were exposed in me that needed help too. Change starts with you—and sometimes it's *you* who needs to change before you can start bringing change to the world around you. What I realized in that moment was that if I wanted to be a positive force in the life of my friend, I needed to work on myself too.

On my flight back I saw a young mom with her daughter. They were calmly sitting together and the mom was teaching the daughter a different language. I was amazed by the grace and patience on display. How could this mom be so calm with her child? What did she have that I didn't? How was she able to enjoy her time with those closest to her in what is often a stressful situation? (Anyone who's traveled with young children knows what I'm talking about!) I was floored. I wanted that. I wanted that ability to show grace and patience with others, even when I feel frustrated, angry, misunderstood, or wronged.

I know grace is always an option. I know that it's possible to show grace because of Jesus. He was whipped, beaten, spit at, and tortured. He died a painful, undeserved death. He was forsaken, abandoned, deserted, and berated. But despite all that, he wasn't bitter. He wasn't angry. He was willing to suffer to bring salvation to all who were lost. And in the middle of his agony, he said, "Father, forgive them, for they don't know what they are doing."[5]

Sometimes, the biggest change we hope to see comes from within. Jesus could have harbored the hatred in his heart. He could have been angry. He could have turned his back on us forever. He could have called a thousand angels to come and rescue him. But he didn't. He had a bigger story to tell. Jesus stayed the course, choosing to die on a cross and bear the full punishment that you and I deserve for the way that we think, act, and treat people. He chose death so that we could live. But it doesn't stop there. Three days later he beat death and rose from the grave. Death, the thing that we fear most, couldn't contain him.

When you understand that death is under God's rule, it changes things. You see people differently. You see situations differently. You see money, time, and resources differently. When you understand that death isn't the end, that is when you truly start to live. You're free to stop basing your happiness on worldly success, free from holding petty grudges, free from believing that right now is all that matters. You start to see your life in the context of eternity.

Life is not easy, and that shouldn't come as a surprise. We live in a broken world, with broken systems, full of broken people. And it's our job to fix the broken world and repair the broken systems, but also to understand that *we* are the broken people. We are the people who have been hurt and have done the hurting. So we need to change. We need to change our thought processes, change our actions, and change our hearts.

I believe that there is a way to heal our broken selves. I believe it in the depths of my soul. I've seen it firsthand. If you believe in Jesus—believe that he is the Son of God, that he came to earth, lived a life without fault, died on a cross, and rose from the dead so that we can live—he can change the course of your life and the course of your family's life. If you believe that he has bought your life with his own, then you no longer need to fear death. He'll save you from yourself, your sin, and the penalty that comes with sin. It's like he hits the Delete button on all your mistakes—past, present, and future. He washes you as white as snow. He removes your sins as far as the east is from the west.

A lot of us don't believe that. We believe that there's no way we can be forgiven for the wrong we've done. Or we believe that there's no way a perfect God would allow evil to happen. That's fair to have those questions. But I would say this: if we want things to change for the better, we need to start with our own hearts. Let's change thought patterns and behaviors, knowing that these changes can have a ripple effect on our broken systems, laws, and societies. Let's build heaven on earth. Let's be the people we wish we had in our lives. Let's become the change that we wish we saw in the world around us.

Without a grace focus, we will never get beyond pointing our fingers at the faults and failings of others. But when we receive the grace and forgiveness that Jesus showed, we can start to experience healing and change in our own hearts. The more we lean into grace, the more we can move beyond anger and frustration and instead approach the broken people and systems around us with an open heart that encourages them to become better.

So I'm learning to work on my heart. To acknowledge and work on my issues, and not focus on other people's faults. I'm learning to show grace—to my family, my friends, and myself. I'm learning to change—because change starts with me.

FOCUS ON LOVE

I had just dropped off my wife and kids at the hair salon and driven to a local library to work on this book. "Are you staying for the play?" someone asked as I walked in. I was intrigued. I grew up doing drama in school and have always loved plays. "It's about Martin Luther King Jr.," the lady continued. I walked into the side room where the play was about to begin. It was amazing. I learned so much about Dr. King. I learned that he was brilliant. I learned that he graduated high school at age fifteen and went to college. I learned that he initially wanted to be a lawyer, not a minister like his dad and granddad. I learned that he moved from Alabama to Tennessee to continue the civil rights movement.

But I also learned other things. I learned that because of some of the laws we have today, some people may not be taught this history. I learned that because of laws back then, Black people weren't allowed to eat at the same restaurants as whites. Legality does not always equal morality. Just because something is legal doesn't mean it's right. What it took then and what it takes now to overcome unjust laws is people doing what's right, even if it breaks the law.

I learned about love that day too. It was so cool. But what was even cooler was Chelsea, one of the actors with Bright Star Touring Theatre, the group that put on the show. At the end she and the other actor were gracious enough to take questions from the audience. I asked them why they do what they do. Chelsea's response: "I want to use my gift to change the world." She's twenty-four. After teaching theater for five years, she decided to start acting professionally. Now she's telling stories like this. Using her voice for good. She loves what she does and loves sharing stories like the one of Dr. King to any audience that will listen. There was a moment in this play where I shed tears, not only because of the story but because of her voice. When she sang, it was no longer a show. It was real life. Her voice reminded me of my childhood. She reminded me of home. I decided to take my oldest son, Caleb, to see their show. It was special. He had so many questions, and I didn't have all the answers. But we're learning to love like Dr. King did. One heart at a time.

If you want to be a changemaker, you must find your focus. Distraction is the enemy. It'll pull you away from your fire. Don't let yourself lose sight of the things that really matter. The people who need your time and attention. The places you can make a difference. The areas where you can bring grace and love.

EIGHT

DREAM IT.
PLAN IT.
DO IT.

Without a vision the people perish.[1] You need a vision. I need a vision. Without one, we're destined to coast along without direction, or wither away instead of growing in the plans and purposes God has for us. Whenever I talk about following the fire, it includes the vision God has given you, your dream for the future. And you can't follow your dream unless you have one.

In college we had this saying on binders, folders, even on T-shirts:

Dream it.
Plan it.
Do it.

I took that to heart. In college I knew my dream: to make it to the NFL. I developed a plan. But the hardest part was doing it. Following the fire is not easy. But it's worth it. Here are some steps I've learned for making your dream a reality.

STEP 1: MAKE TIME TO DREAM

The first step to having a dream is making space for one. We live in a society that's always on the go. We need to take more time to think, plan, and evaluate. Instead of rushing into the next thing, let's plan a bit. I have a friend who runs a sports team. He was looking for a new coach and wanted to get it right. The only issue was, many people in that industry believe you have to rush the decision, to move quickly rather than correctly. But this friend of mine wanted to take a different approach. He wanted to take the time to play the right note. He employed a search team, asked for advice, and took the time to get it right. His decision paid off. He made the right call, and he made it on his time frame, not someone else's. Making time to dream isn't just important for owners of sports teams; it's important for you and me too.

We have to take some time to think about what it is we want to accomplish, who it is we want to be. "Write the vision; make it plain on tablets, so he may run who reads it."[2] So take the time, write the vision. Give yourself space to dream. For me, giving myself space looks like taking a walk—often in the morning—to spend time with God, finding a quiet place with my pen, a pad, and sometimes my Bible. There's something about the stillness of the morning before life gets going, that space in your mind that hasn't yet been filled by the worries of the day. That time is special. Whether you're in a position to go out in nature, or you need to find a corner of your house or apartment, take advantage of that time. You would be surprised by what dreams start with a simple, quiet thought. Dream it.

STEP 2: BELIEVE IN YOUR DREAM

Your dream may seem crazy, but it's yours. Believe in it. You may have dreams of tens of millions, or you may have dreams of ten. No matter what your dream is, believe in it. If you don't believe, no one else will. My dad is still dreaming of houses and hotels, more wings to the hospital. He never stops dreaming!

It's crazy how some of his dreams happen. I remember first hearing about the hospital he was hoping to build in Nigeria. He said it would cost over 200 million naira (that's over half a million dollars). We didn't have the money. But he kept on dreaming. He brought the entire team of missionaries and showed them the land where the hospital would be built. One of the missionaries actually took a piece of dirt from that land in a small bag (still not sure if that's legal), brought it back to America, and prayed over it every day.

Eighteen months later, after two nominations for the Walter Payton NFL Man of the Year award, a wildly successful charity event, and a few generous donors, the hospital was built. What was once dirt now brings life. Believe in your dream.

When we were working on building the Austin Harvest food mart on the West Side, we needed to raise half a million dollars. For whatever reason, I believed. Two weeks and seventeen people later, the money was raised. Miracles happen when you believe. There's a story in the Bible of a boy who was demon possessed. Since his childhood this boy hadn't been right. Until he met Jesus. After a bit of conversation, and the inability of the disciples to help the boy, Jesus met the boy's dad with a question.

"And He asked [the boy's] father, 'How long has this been happening to him?' And he said, 'From childhood. It has often thrown him both into the fire and into the water to kill him. But *if You can do anything*, take pity on us and help us!'" The father had heard about Jesus. He knew about his miracles, knew about his power, but there was still a little doubt. Jesus called him out on it: "'If You can?' All things are possible for the one who believes."[3] I love how direct Jesus' statement is. There's no doubt, no confusion in his words and tone.

All things are possible to him who believes.

The story could end there, but it doesn't. "Immediately the boy's father cried out and said, 'I do believe; help my unbelief!'"[4] I believe this story is an example for us. An example for those who semi-believe, who *almost* believe. *Lord, I do believe, but help my unbelief.* A simple yet powerful prayer. Jesus would go on to heal the boy, but I believe the father was also changed forever. Miracles will do that to you. So will believing. Believe in your dream.

STEP 3: KEEP YOUR DREAM
IN A SAFE SPACE

Dreams can be fragile. You don't want to throw them around anywhere. Keep them in a safe place, written down and with trusted people.

When my friend brought that dirt back from Nigeria, he didn't flaunt it around everywhere for the world to see. He kept it on a desk in his house as a reminder of where he had been and where he was going. That dirt served as a reminder of what he believed God was going to do. And now it serves as a reminder of what God *did* do. Every time my friend looks at that dirt, he remembers that dreams can come true. He remembers

Dreams can be fragile. You don't want to throw them around anywhere. Keep them in a safe place, written down and with trusted people.

when there was just dirt at the site of the hospital. He still comes to the hospital every year. Even after a bad back injury, he's committed to the mission. He's spent too much time dreaming to let a little back pain stop him. He's seen miracles happen.

When I had the dream of making it to the NFL and it finally hit me that this dream could be a reality, I made the mistake of sharing it too early. "Don't get your hopes up," people would say. "You know it's nearly impossible." After a while I started to believe them. Then I remembered the words that I'm writing here today. Your dream is not for everyone. So keep it safe. Hide it in your heart. Dream it, plan it, do it, and let God do the rest. After that moment, I didn't share the dream with anyone. I didn't want others' doubts to seep into my thinking and planning and striving. The same thing happened when I was getting ready to marry my wife. God had made it abundantly clear that this woman was the one. I wasn't ready for people to cast doubt over God's decision. Those two critical decisions in my life were kept safe. They still needed a bit of protection.

If you have a dream, keep it safe for a little while, until it can really take root and withstand the naysayers and doubters who inevitably show up when a dreamer speaks up.

STEP 4: ALLOW YOUR DREAM TO GROW

Keeping your dream in a safe place doesn't mean hiding it. Give it light and water. Don't stuff it away. Do things that will help accomplish your dream. Give yourself opportunities and put yourself in places and spaces that can help it come true.

It took around five years from the time the dream of the hospital was spoken to the hospital actually being built, but my father had been dreaming about it for far longer. The organization that eventually founded the hospital started in 1988. The dream was spoken in 2013. The hospital wasn't built until 2018. Thirty years. It took time for others to believe in what my dad was doing. It took time for *him* to believe! It took time for the dream to develop. Though your dream may take time, don't give up on it. It will happen. You may just have to start out with some dirt.

When I was first thinking about playing football in college or even professionally, I initially didn't believe I'd be able to survive the grueling practices and intense training regimen. I thought I needed killer instincts, and sometimes I wasn't sure I was made of the right stuff. I questioned whether I'd faced enough pain and struggle to have what it took to accomplish great things.

But I was wrong. There's more than one way to

develop a dream. Pain is often a precedent, but there is a universal building block behind every dream before it becomes a reality: progress.

Some people simply desire to be better today than they were yesterday, and they take that mentality into everything they do in life. That's me.

Some people just want to compete. That's me.

Some people just want to achieve beyond their wildest dreams. That's me too.

I didn't grow up in Nigeria. I didn't have to go to a stream to fetch water, or walk miles to school every day, or go to work immediately after. But I did experience my own pain and my own progress. Whatever path you've been on—whether it's been full of pain, or privilege, or a mix of the two—know that you have what you need to take that next step toward your dream.

STEP 5: PLAN HOW TO ACCOMPLISH YOUR DREAM

Write down your plan. You'd be surprised how much gets done by simply writing something down. Work on that plan and watch your dream get accomplished.

People have asked me how I was able to do so much in college—graduate with an honors degree, win the

William V. Campbell trophy (nicknamed the "Academic Heisman"), start for a football team that went to the national championship, and make it to the NFL. I'll tell you the secret: It was all about time management. I had to learn how to manage my time well. I wrote things down, did them, and checked them off my list, day after day after day. This practice may seem simple, but it was extremely effective. It helped me reach daily goals—mini goals that are the foundation for reaching bigger goals.

I have a friend named David. He's a dad, a husband, and a pretty good TV analyst as well. But he wants to be better. So every day David writes down three things that he wants to do or be for his family. He recently gave me an example. "(1) Compliment more than I criticize today (and out-compliment my wife). (2) Serve three different people today. Do something for them and ask for nothing in return. (3) Tell my daughter, multiple times, how beautiful she is and how much I value her." Those were his goals for one day. Now multiply that by 365.

Impact.

I recently started following his lead and implementing daily goals myself. I'll give you an example: "(1) See my kids how God sees them. See them for who they are. (2) Serve my wife well today. Help her at every turn. (3) Hang out with my family. No agenda, no homework, just hang. Spend today with them.

Change starts with
your daily decision
to be a different
person today than
you were yesterday.

Multiply that daily list, stretching it across weeks, months, a full year. *Impact. Change.*

Change does not have to be massive, high-profile accomplishments or far-off goals. But you do have to be intentional. Change starts with your daily decision to be a different person today than you were yesterday.

STEP 6: JUST DO IT

This book is for me. Let me tell you why. You've been reading about all of these dreamers, these builders, the waymakers and risk-takers.

But even as I write this book I still struggle with believing that I am, in fact, capable of dreaming big. Maybe that's just reserved for the ones who do it all the time, the ones who have done it before. The ones I'm writing about.

If you're like me, you need to remind yourself often: Don't buy into the lie that only a select few are allowed to dream. If you've listened to that lie and allowed it to shape you and direct you to a place that's far from your dreams, maybe you need to remember who you used to be. I had to do that. I went through a season when I needed to take some time to think, pray, process, and remember who I used to be. How I used to dream. How I used to think.

I reconnected with my high school self, who wanted so deeply to see the world become a better place. Who wanted those who were forsaken to be loved and cared for. I remembered being in college and wanting to use my platform, my influence, for the benefit of others. I remembered being in the professional world and praying that people would see the inherent value they have in themselves. I remembered dreaming. Somewhere along the way, I stopped dreaming. I stopped believing big things. I stopped believing the impossible. Maybe you did too. It's not too late to go back.

In Nigerian culture there's a phrase that goes, "You know where the towel is—pick it up and run with it." Basically it means, "It's never too late to keep on going. You know exactly where you dropped your task—pick it up and keep going! Start again! Now is the perfect time." For me, the phrase is a reminder that you know the point where you left your dreams. You know the time when they died. You know exactly when you stopped dreaming. That's a fact. But another reality is that you, yes you, have the power to go back to that place, pick up the towel, and run with it.

After a conversation with a friend and a few freeing tears, I began being who God made me to be. I started bringing all my gifts to bear. I used my position in the sports world to connect athletes to causes they cared about. I saw players and coaches who were hurting, and I started bringing healing. I addressed the broken-ness within myself. I moved from words to actions and began to believe. God did the rest. I'm still in the process of letting God change me. I'm getting curious and staying open.

Your dreams are there for the taking. Just do it. Even when you're tired. Even when sleep is knocking on your door. There's a verse I call to mind whenever I'm tempted to procrastinate, to wait until tomorrow to do something that I know I could do today. "A little sleep, a little slumber, a little folding of the hands to rest," and poverty sneaks up on you.[5] Don't sleep on your dreams.

If you're feeling overwhelmed by the magnitude of your dream and feel intimidated by the advice to "just do it," let me fill you in on a secret. You don't have to do all of it at once. In fact, the bigger and more worthwhile the dream is, the less likely you'll be able to accomplish it overnight. If that's where you find yourself, "just do it" might mean focusing on the little things you can do, the stuff that's right in front of you.

I had a coach who once said, "Little things done well make big things happen." This quote, which is attributed to John Wooden, the famed basketball coach, is a reminder that greatness on the football field isn't about a monumental effort in the heat of the moment; it's about doing the little things well, day after day after day. The truth is that for every moment of inspired in-game heroics that you see on TV, there were hundreds or thousands of hours of practicing the fundamentals.

The same truth applies in life. Change happens in leaps and bounds but also in crawls and waddles. It starts with the little things. For me, my greatest seasons came after I spent an extra fifteen minutes a day working on my craft. I didn't notice the change, but over time others did. My footwork was better, as was my technique. I worked on my eyes, processing the split-second moments that make a difference between executing well or failing. I practiced the little things. I'd recommend giving this method a try in your everyday life. The little things add up. Little things done well make big things happen.

You are the only one who can accomplish your dreams. It may take you making that call you've been putting off. It may take you asking for help. It may take you offering help. But it takes you—your presence, your focus, and your action.

Dream it. Plan it. Do it.

NINE

FIND YOUR TEAM

found myself on stage in front of the biggest crowd before the biggest game of the year, and it all started with saying yes. The Athletes in Action Super Bowl Breakfast is one of the biggest events of Super Bowl week. The week of the Super Bowl is fun. It's full of people and parties, events and entertainment. But the biggest moment for me was at breakfast. I had shown up to this year's Super Bowl not with the NFL or ESPN but with another acronym: IJM.

I mentioned International Justice Mission in an earlier chapter, along with my opportunity to visit Guatemala for a few days. IJM is a global organization combating human trafficking and modern-day slavery, with twenty-nine field offices in seventeen countries. IJM's goal is to protect half a billion vulnerable people by 2030.

Here's how they operate. Certain countries have a broken justice system. Because of that, the bad guys consistently get away with crime. Police abuse power, community members steal land, women and children are exploited. With a broken justice system, there's no one to stop the bad guys from committing these crimes. That's

where IJM comes in. The team at IJM works with partners and law enforcement to equip local lawyers, judges,
social workers, and justice systems with the necessary
tools to prosecute the bad guys. Sometimes all these
countries need is a hotline. A phone number that people
can call to report abuse. Other times it's something more
complex. Maybe it's a new system of tracking perpetra-
tors. Maybe it's a safe haven for women and children who
have been abused. Maybe it's more. Whatever the details
of that region's injustice, IJM comes in, learns as much as
they can, and equips local leaders in any way they need.

I initially learned about IJM at a conference I
attended. I had heard about the work, but life seemed a
bit too busy to get heavily involved. And then, suddenly,
it wasn't. I received an opportunity through the NFL
Players Association to participate in an externship, with
a list of companies and cities to choose from. IJM was
on the list of potential organizations and the opportunity was in a city I had been hoping to visit, so I was in.
I embarked on my journey to Washington, DC, thinking I would go, spend a week, learn a little, then leave.

Boy was I in for an awakening. When I arrived at
IJM's headquarters, I met a team of dedicated people.
People who were determined to make a change not
only in their community but also in communities all
around the world. I met men and women, young and

old, focused on helping the hurting and protecting the vulnerable. They had no superpowers, they were not superhuman; they were everyday people who had made a decision that enough was enough.

After that week, I was sold. This organization cared about all the things that mattered to me. It was international, it cared about fixing broken systems, and to top it all off, they wanted to give me opportunities to speak. I became part of an ambassador program and got to speak on behalf of IJM. It was a dream come true.

But before living the dream, I had to experience the nightmare.

NOT ALL HEROES WEAR CAPES

It was the middle of the summer and I found myself in Guatemala City, Guatemala, with IJM. In high school I had memorized all the Central American countries and their capitals, but I had never visited. I knew *about* these places, but I didn't really *know* them. Visiting Guatemala gave me a whole new perspective. I learned about the complicated history that Guatemala has with America. I learned about the CIA operation in 1954 that overthrew a democratically elected government in Guatemala and caused chaos in the country for decades. I learned about

They had no
superpowers,
they were not
superhuman; they
were everyday
people who had
made a decision that
enough was enough.

the period from 1962 to 1996 when the US provided weapons, training, and aid to a Guatemalan government that was terrorizing civilians. I learned about some complicated history that Guatemala has with itself—the roots of the racism and classism that exist in that country. I went to burial grounds and businesses, safe havens and sanctuaries. I learned. But I also saw. I saw children who had been abused. Women who were scared for their lives. I was heartbroken.

One particular situation hit me especially hard: meeting with children who were sexual assault survivors. This group of young girls and boys had been brave enough to share their stories with someone who could help. They had been bold enough to speak about what had happened, knowing it could change the course of their lives and their families' lives forever. They had been strong enough to realize that it wasn't their fault, that they were not the problem.

Sometimes you will experience being used or abused. Mocked or made fun of. Left out or laughed at. It's not your fault. What happened to you is not your fault. It never was, no matter what you've been telling yourself or what you've been told. These children taught me that firsthand.

One by one the children came up. They gave their names and told us about their favorite things to do and foods to eat. They stood on stage, smiled with joy, and shared their lives with us. They allowed us to come up, one by one, and they gave us a gift. A handwritten picture card, beautifully designed by them. After that we sat together and ate lunch with them. We laughed, we joked, and I stumbled through my limited Spanish to make a connection. I was in the presence of kings and queens. These children had been through tremendous heartache and unimaginable pain. Yet they were speaking up and speaking out. They were seeking justice through their own sadness and pain. They were heroes.

I left Guatemala with a newfound purpose. It took me a while to process that purpose and the emotions that came with it. I kept remembering those children who had become my friends, seeing their smiles and joy despite the suffering they'd been through.

That's why during Super Bowl week I spent time on several stages speaking on behalf of IJM, on behalf of those kids. We were giving away Super Bowl tickets in exchange for sign-ups. There were fourteen hundred people at the event. Over half of the attendees submitted their emails. That's a good start. But there are so many people who need protection and rescuing. We need *everyone* to sign up. There may not be a promise of a Super Bowl ticket, but there is a promise of being able to save someone from a sordid situation. It's pretty sobering.

For those who want to learn more, go to ijm.org. Join the fight. Become a superhero.

SOY UN HÉROE

I mentioned that we held a special ceremony for the sexual abuse survivors. This ceremony was an opportunity for us to celebrate these children for their bravery. We gave them pins that read, "Soy un héroe," which means "I'm a hero." That ceremony was special. We celebrated these brave boys and girls and thanked them for their heroism. They even wore superhero capes to signify their bravery. I will never forget that moment. Below is a poem I wrote a few days after leaving Guatemala, inspired by the memory of a young girl I was able to give a hero pin to. A young girl who had shared her story and helped capture her abuser.

> Not all superheroes wear capes, but
>> most do.
> Heroes come in different shapes and sizes.
> From different contexts and backgrounds.
> Some are small. So small.
> So small that you wouldn't think their cape
>> would fit them. It fits just fine.

Not all heroes wear capes, but most do.
Heroes are chosen. But in the most
      inconspicuous of ways.
They are chosen by God to fight a battle
      that would have killed someone else.
Not all heroes wear capes.

Not all heroes wear capes, but most do.
A hero is a person who often doesn't see
      themselves as a hero.
They carry a burden so heavy that it often
      feels unbearable.
Not all heroes wear capes.

Not all heroes wear capes, but most do.
I met my heroes on a trip out of the country.
A trip I didn't want to go on.
My hero is much smaller than me.
She's much younger than me as well.
Not all heroes wear capes, but most do.

The reason I share all of this about how I came to be involved with IJM is that sometimes we hit a point in our journey of dream-building and changemaking when we realize we need a team. A group of likeminded people who've come together to do something bigger than any one person could accomplish alone. Sometimes you get to be a founder, someone who starts something brand new based on your own vision and dream. But sometimes you get to jump on board with a dream that's already in motion. At IJM I found a group of people whose passions, goals, and purpose lined up with my own. They helped me discover a new way of following my fire.

INVEST IN PEOPLE

Chase relationships, not opportunity. Seek love in real life, not likes on social media. Invest in people. Your dream isn't just about you. It may start with you, but it doesn't end there.

A friend of mine and I were having a conversation. He was frustrated with himself because though he had built a successful business, he had worked his people into the ground. He had made a lot of money but few friends. He had been using his gifts for his own glory. The interesting thing about this story is that my friend actually gave away a huge portion of his profits to charity. He loved this aspect of his company. They were able to help thousands of people around the world have better lives and build better communities. But the people here at home, his family and his employees, were paying the price. He was discouraged. While we were talking, he described his love for building businesses, getting deals, and making money—all with the purpose of doing good in the world. And he was talented at it. But he was alone. He had stepped on anyone who got in the way of his goals.

I knew what that was like. When he dropped me off at the airport, I gave him a hug. And then words came out of my mouth.

"You have unique skills and abilities to build. They just need to be redirected. Keep on building—build like crazy. But build people, not businesses. Build people."

I don't know where these words were from. But I know they were for him.

I've had friends who have moved from one side of the country to another—for people. I've had mentors who have quit their jobs and started nonprofits—for people. I've even had friends work twice as hard at their jobs and show up when they didn't have to—for people. So use your gifts to build people; the business will follow.

CHANGE STARTS WITH US

The biggest lesson I learned about myself during my time in the NFL is that though I value teams, I don't always like being a part of them. I like doing things my own way and marching to the beat of my own drum, at my own pace. But I'm learning that if I want to be full and walk in purpose, it has to be done with others.

When I played on teams, each team member had a different role. Coaches too. A starting quarterback's job is to run the offense. To pass the ball to his receivers and hand it off to his running back. The backup's job is a bit different. It's to be ready to step in if needed, but also to help the starter maintain a high level of game-readiness. Third string's job is also supportive, focusing on watching film and bringing insights to the starter's preparation. Each has their role.

On the defensive side, an outside linebacker's job is to make sure no one runs around the outside of the defense. An inside linebacker's job is to cover running backs, make tackles, and communicate the calls to the defensive line. The defensive line's job is to make sure no one runs up the middle and to wreak havoc on an offense. Safeties and corners have jobs too. Each position, starting and backup, has a role to play. And when that role is executed properly, you win. But you can't win alone.

When I retired from the NFL and began my career in speaking and broadcasting, I tried to do it alone. It wasn't working. I'd get burned, taken advantage of, or

If we, as a people,

want to survive,

we have to survive

together. Two are

better than one.

Change starts with us.

feel incomplete. But now I'm learning to trust, finding my team beyond the NFL setting. It's hard, but I'm learning.

I have a friend who I'm learning to trust. We are as different as night and day. He's a thinker, I'm a doer. He evaluates, I jump. He thinks seventeen steps ahead, I take things one day at a time. I love to do things on my own, but I need my friend. I need his insight; I need his guidance. I need his wisdom. And he needs me too. He needs my joy. He needs my love. We need each other. However, my friend and I each tend to do things alone. I'm changing that. If we, as a people, want to survive, we have to survive together. Two are better than one. Change starts with us.

TEN

FOLLOW THE FIRE—
BUT DON'T BURN OUT

God can outdream you. He can take you to places you could never imagine in your wildest dreams. I've written this book to help you realize that there is a reason why you are on this earth, a reason why you exist. I want to help you take the time to find that reason and follow it, knowing and believing that real change is possible through simple faithfulness to following the dream God has put on your heart.

But what does it look like when your dream starts to ignite, when the fire starts to catch? What happens after you've committed to the motivational message I shared in the previous chapters? When you've found your fire, started saying yes, gathered your architects, taken some concrete steps, and the dream is starting to become a reality? In this chapter I want to share a few things about my own experiences that might help you navigate your journey.

PUSH PAST THE EARLY DOUBTS AND FEARS

As I shared earlier, sometimes you just have to start building. If you wait until every possible next step has been considered, planned, and decided, you'll never actually take the first step! Sometimes it's as simple as looking at your passions, identifying a way those passions can be expressed, and just starting.

I love talking and wanted to learn more about justice, so I took what seemed like a good first step: I started a podcast. I didn't have a specific guest list. Anyone who texted me was likely next week's guest! My producer didn't love that, but it worked. As we got going, I started making a list of people I wanted on the show. But if they were busy or unresponsive, I just let it happen. I learned so much from that podcast. I learned from authors and artists, professors and pro athletes. It was special. But I nearly never started.

I was afraid of starting a podcast. But thankfully, I had a good friend who reminded me to go for it. I was afraid of the consistency that would be required, afraid about developing the content, afraid that people wouldn't listen. I was full of fear. I think I was also afraid because I didn't want to fail. I didn't want to start something and not finish it.

I wanted this to be the best podcast ever. I cared a lot about the result. What I forgot about was the journey. Looking back now, about six months after the final episode of that season, I realize that starting a podcast was never about the destination. It was always about

Fall in love with
the process. Follow
the thing you're in
love with. Just get
started. You will
feel fear. You might
be hesitant. Keep
going. Try it anyway.

the journey, the process. Fall in love with the process. Follow the thing you're in love with. Just get started. You will feel fear. You might be hesitant. Keep going. Try it anyway. It may not work. You may get through only one season or just a few episodes. But what you will learn along the journey is priceless.

DON'T BE SURPRISED BY DISCOURAGEMENT

If you're working toward change, especially toward changing serious injustice, I can tell you right now that you're going to face discouragement. After the death of Walter Scott, another Black man killed here in America, I was both discouraged and confused. I had a meeting planned with two individuals to record an episode of the podcast. The interview was to be with two Black men who both cared about justice and wanted to make a change. But after this tragedy, none of us were feeling it. We decided to reschedule. Our hearts were too heavy in that moment.

Grief is a process. Loss weighs on people differently. So does injustice. People process loss, pain, and fear on their own timeline. I had to learn that firsthand. Sometimes you need a break. And that's okay. Listen to your body. Get some rest. Collect your thoughts. Every event doesn't require your response. You don't have to be an expert. Even if you are an expert, it's wise to take a break every now and then. Rest.

Change is never easy. Discouragement is. It's okay to be discouraged, but don't stop at discouragement. Share your fears and your feelings with your friends. Share your doubts with those closest to you. But make sure they're listening.

I was recently having a conversation with my brother. He was sharing with me an idea that he was really excited about. All of a sudden I started to critique it. I noticed what I believed were some flaws in his plan and wanted to make sure he considered them. As I spoke, I noticed that his mood began to change. Emmanuel is a thinker. He's a brilliant strategist with grand visions, but he wasn't quite feeling my feedback. So before I continued, I asked him a simple question: "Do you want me to keep on going?" He didn't. His idea was still in the early stages. The last thing he needed was someone saying why it wouldn't work. So I stopped. We continued our dinner and left that conversation at the table. It was as if it was unwanted food that the server picked up. That moment wasn't the time, but it taught me something: even those closest to you may not know what you're going through. They may not understand your vision. So share it only with someone who can add fuel to it. Or don't share it at all.

People may not get where you're trying to go. They may have already tried and failed to do something similar, and they assume you will try and fail too. That's a wrong assumption. Hold your hopes with care. Protect them. Care for them. Your dream may be the one to change your situation, but it's delicate. It's precious and needs to be nurtured.

When I was trying to make a positive impact on the city of Chicago, people thought I was crazy. But I didn't. I shared my dream with a few trusted loved ones, and they added fuel to my fire. I remember always wanting to go to a place where I could make an impact. When I heard about an opportunity to come to Chicago, I got excited because there was diversity. I got excited because there was an opportunity. I got excited because there was a problem that I felt I could help solve. I ran to the fire. And the journey was great. I went to prisons and police ride-alongs, visited politicians and preschools. It was so much fun. I learned so much. That's something people don't tell you: Being a changemaker may be hard, but it's also fun. You experience a ton.

REMEMBER WHO YOU ARE

I recently decided to spend more time trying to study the Bible. Early in my life I memorized a lot of scriptures.

Then I stopped. I stopped because I didn't realize how good I had it. I didn't realize that I was already doing the best thing. I was spending my time wisely. It wasn't until I got away from it that I realized how much I was missing it. Missing my time with my weapon.

See, there's a spiritual battle going on. A battle of the mind. A battle of courage versus discouragement. Faith versus fear. There's a constant battle trying to keep us from our purpose. And I was losing this battle. It wasn't until I spent time with a friend and realized that the aura that I used to provide, I wasn't able to provide anymore. I wasn't being me. I wasn't being loving and kind, thoughtful and full of energy. I needed to be reminded of me.

I was recently on a Zoom call with friends. We meet weekly and talk about life. But they noticed something. They noticed that early on in our talk, my heart was heavy. I was grieving. As the call went on, and as I continued to open up in front of these trusted loved ones, the weight seemed to be lifted. I began to tell a story to them about things that brought me joy. At the end of my soliloquy, a friend of mine called me out. She called out the best in me. "Sam, *that* is you. That's the real Sam. You lit up when you were telling us the story about your wife and the cake and your kids. And I want you to know that it's okay to have both. It's okay to feel the messiness of the mourning and the joy of the journey.

It's okay to hold both. It's okay to feel." That's when the tears arrived.

This friend of mine, this trusted confidant, saw me in my weakness and called out the best in me. I left that meeting feeling freer than I had before, freer than I had in weeks. It's okay to mourn. It's okay to take steps forward and take steps backward. It's even okay to not move at all. It's okay to be alone. But it's not okay to stay alone. It's never okay to stay alone. That's when the discouragement kicks in.

So, as my friends and I were figuring out what to do with the most recent injustice we had witnessed, as we were figuring out what to do with our thoughts, ideas, and emotions, as we were journeying together, we paused. We mourned. We went in different directions. We used what we had. My friend A. D. "Lumkile" Thomason wrote a book, *Permission to Be Black*. I started a podcast. My other friend accepted a promotion at a Fortune 500 company. We all used what we had. We all went back and forth. We all journeyed.

The journey may not always go exactly how you planned. In fact, it rarely will. You'll start, you'll stop, you'll go backward, you'll make progress. Don't give up. Remember who you are. Stay faithful to the identity and purpose God has given you.

FOLLOW THE FIRE—BUT DON'T BURN OUT!

There will always be more work to do, but I'm trying to learn how to rest. I'm trying to learn how to finish. I've worked hard in life. I continue to work hard. But it's important to stop and take joy in what you've achieved. There's freedom in being finished with a task and then enjoying the fruits of your labor. Those times between the tasks, between reaching one dream and then embarking on another, are meant to restore and recharge you. For example, during certain seasons of life, I was so busy and focused that I didn't really have space to just spend time with people and enjoy community. But people fuel me. Hanging out with my friends and family ignites me. It keeps me from burning out. I need that. You do too.

Rest looks different for different people. It can look like taking a day out of the week and doing nothing related to work. It can look like taking an hour or two out of the day and going to get a workout in. It can look like taking a few weeks out of the year and doing nothing, or maybe going somewhere special. Whatever you're working on now, focus on finishing it well. But don't neglect to think about how you'll rest once you reach that goal. I'm a doer, and sometimes I feel that if I stop running, I'll fall behind. I've never felt finished. But rest is important. In fact, it's both a gift and a command from God. At the very beginning of the Scripture, we read that God rested after the work of creation. And that same pattern of work and rest was built into God's laws for the people of Israel.[1]

Finding Balance

In this book I've focused a lot on finding the things that drive you and following them. It's about taking action. But it's also important that you discover how to balance your drives. Without balance, a positive drive can take a negative turn.

When I was in second grade, I wrote my first book, *The Boy Who Disobeyed*. It was a project that all of the second graders did. You could choose to write about any topic you wanted: sports stars, action figures, superheroes. I chose to write about myself. I wrote about the me who wanted to do *all* the fun things. Who wanted to go out and play with his friends at the playground, kick the soccer ball, and play with his toys even when his parents said it was time to put them away. I wrote about obedience, but then I disobeyed. In the book, drawings included, I portrayed myself sneaking out of the house through the window in the room that my brother and I shared (I know, I would make a bad witness). I drew myself walking outside and going to the playground and seeing some friends. I drew myself pushing them on the swing and us playing basketball together. But then it was getting late, and I needed to get home. So I drew myself walking home by myself, kicking a can, thinking of how I would make it back to my house without my parents noticing. I climbed back through the window and into my room. I'd succeeded in doing what I wanted—but instead of feeling happy in the story, I began to cry. I felt ashamed. Nobody knew what I had done in my imaginary story, but I did. The story closed with my confession to my parents, their disappointment, and me getting punished and feeling sad.

I was seven when I wrote and illustrated this surprisingly heavy story about obedience, expectations, guilt, and shame! At a very young age I had a keen understanding of right and wrong, but I also was driven by a desire to please. And that desire to obey and please my parents ran right up against the things I wanted to do. To not clean up my toys after playing. To not help clean up the kitchen.

Just recently I was sitting with a life planner. This is an individual you sit with and, you guessed it, plan out your life. About halfway through our two-day meeting he asked me a question. "Sam, what percentage of time do you spend doing what someone else wants you to do versus what you want you to do?"

"Ninety-five percent," I replied.

"I figured that," he responded. "If you keep that up, you'll end up curled in a ball somewhere. And I don't want that."

Neither did I. I needed to find my fire and follow it. I knew where I had dropped the ball, and now I was ready to pick it up again. For so long I had been achieving, but I had been missing out on finding the balance.

Part of what makes balance so hard to find is that often our dreams are incredibly good, praiseworthy things. And that's why it can be hard to recognize that there's a problem when they've become all-consuming. Here's an example of what I mean. I'm devoted to the goal of loving people well. When my life planner and I talked about my *opus gloria*, the words I want people to say at my funeral, what I want to be known for, it was easy for me to pick it out: "Sam loved me well."

No one could say that goal is a bad thing. Jesus himself prioritized loving people as second only to loving God. But with the way I'm wired (including the built-in desire to please others), pursuing that goal can make me intensely focused on others, pouring out my time and energy to make the lives of other people better. When I'm praised for that work, I'm motivated to throw myself even harder into the next project. But I'm absolutely crushed if I feel that I haven't done enough.

That's where burnout starts to set in, where my focus on a praiseworthy goal starts tipping toward imbalance.

Slow Down

Jesus was never in a rush, but we are. Sometimes I wonder why. I wonder why we're so caught up in the next career goal that we put our friends and family aside. I wonder why we're so obsessed with success that we forget about purpose. I fear that we're missing the point. Slow down. Go to counseling. Confess your sins to one another. Enjoy what you have. That's what my new friend did.

Another friend of mine is a coach for a major college football team. It had been his dream for as long as he could remember, and early in his career he would sacrifice anything—including his family—to achieve this success. Everything changed when his wife was diagnosed with cancer. I couldn't imagine what someone must feel when they or a loved one gets diagnosed with cancer. When I heard my friend share his story, it put everything into perspective.

"All of my goals changed," he began. "I put my family first. I realized that they had been sacrificing for me, and now it was time for me to sacrifice for them." But something else cool happened to my friend. He redefined success. He realized that he could be present

Give yourself grace,
you're almost there.
You're growing and
you're going places.
But give yourself the
grace and time to find
balance along the way.

as a husband and father and have that be considered a success. He reordered his priorities. He would continue to coach and eventually become one of the youngest head coaches in all of college football. His wife would also become cancer-free.

I understand everyone's story does not end that way. I also understand that this friend of mine's story is not over. Neither is mine. We are all rewriting our stories, but perspective is everything. As I was leaving for the day, I went to tell this coach thank you. That was when he reminded me of an important truth. After I thanked him for his time, he said this: "Just think about how many people want to be sitting in your seat right now. Enjoy the heck out of it. Be grateful. You're fortunate." So are you. Change your perspective. Arrange your priorities. You may just be shooting at the wrong goal.

Be kind to yourself. Love others well, but love yourself well too. Give yourself grace, you're almost there. You're growing and you're going places. But give yourself the grace and time to find balance along the way.

Enjoy the successes. Take time between dreams to be fully present with the people God has put in your life.

Don't let your fire burn out. Stay intentional about making room for the things that reignite your fire when you've spent everything you've got pursuing the dreams God has put on your heart.

ELEVEN

WHEN YOUR
DREAM IGNITES

When I played my last game in the National Football League, no one else knew I was done with football, but I did. Over the span of a few months, I'd started to realize that God had a bigger purpose for my life than just to play in the NFL. I wanted to speak, I wanted to encourage. I wanted to be with my family. I wanted to travel. So I had to say no to football. But saying no was harder than I initially anticipated.

A TURNING POINT

The process of saying no to the NFL and saying yes to my future was an arduous one. It all started in a hotel shortly after signing with the Buffalo Bills in the late summer of 2019. It was the day of the second preseason game. I was in my room watching ESPN when a story aired about a young girl in London with a disability. This disability made it hard for her to walk, but even harder for her to get up after a fall—nearly impossible. The kids at her school found out about this disability and bullied her incessantly. They would push her on the ground at recess and leave her unaccompanied, without help. Unless a teacher noticed she wasn't in class and went out to help her, she would be stuck. Students did this day after day after day. I was livid. I began to cry, by myself in my hotel room. Thankfully this story had a happy ending.

Someone at ESPN had caught wind of this girl's plight and decided to look into how they could help. They discovered that this girl was a huge fan of wrestling. She specifically loved Roman Reigns of the WWE. When Roman found out about this girl, he used his gifts for good. Roman and the WWE flew this young girl out to one of their shows and had her not only meet the wrestlers but also join them in the ring. It was a blast.

That's when the tears flowed even more. I couldn't stop crying. It was at that moment when I knew my football career was over. Not because of the crying but because of the calling. I'd known for a long time that I cared deeply about helping people. This story on ESPN—and my reaction to it—made it clear to me that it was time for me to move in that direction. I wanted to do more of that kind of work. I wanted to bring people hope. I wanted to make people feel alive. I just needed to figure out how.

My time with the Buffalo Bills ended up being very short. I got cut from the team before the regular season began, and I started to go through a process. My heart was ready to go, but my mind had yet to rationalize these feelings. My priorities had changed. I was older, wiser, and mentally prepared for a change. But emotionally I was a wreck. I spent the next two months in that hotel room with my wife and kids. And even though I knew it was time to start thinking about life after football, I was experiencing a lot of pressure and stress. Honestly, I felt crushed. I was trying to reconcile myself to the fact that I would be stepping away from a game that had been my life for so many years.

But in the midst of the pressure, I started to find peace. I'm used to being recognized—whether for my size or my smile, something about me usually stands out. But there in that hotel where no one knew my name or recognized my face, I found enough quiet and solitude to connect with God. I ended up staying in that hotel room until November. Praying about my future and processing my emotions.

FREE TO FLY

"Why don't you just retire?" a friend of mine asked me, knowing that I was struggling to find my next step. I was shocked. Though I was pretty sure I was supposed to stop playing football sooner rather than later, it was hard for me to face the possibility of retirement. This game had been a part of my identity for two decades. I was mourning. Though he suggested retirement, his words offered another perspective. What if I could still play, but with different parameters? What if I could play just a bit longer, purely for the joy of the game? And that's what I ended up doing. I was signed by the Tampa Bay Buccaneers and played the last eight games of the 2019–20 season there. I got to enjoy the game of football one last time. Playing time or stats didn't matter. I used that time to mentor younger players and lead the team well. It was the perfect way to let go of the NFL while also getting a preview of the new direction I was headed in, with a focus on serving those around me.

When the season ended I had an exit interview with the head coach. I was pretty sure I was done with the NFL. But I didn't want to be *told* that I was done. Minutes before the exit interview, I felt nervous. This happens sometimes before a big moment; fear and anxiety will begin to creep in. My football future was seemingly in the hands of another human. I felt like I had no control. I'd sensed that it was time to say no to the NFL, but I didn't want to be told no. And then God showed up. I felt the Holy Spirit prompting me, telling me that instead of worrying about what this coach would do or say, I needed to pray.

I found a quiet corner and said a quick prayer. I don't recall exactly what I said, but I know what I heard as a response: *You're going to play as long as* you *want to play.* I suddenly felt such peace, knowing that God was in control. With that, I walked into the meeting. I felt free. Though I hadn't played a ton that year with the Buccaneers, the coach said that he loved the leadership I provided to the team. He knew who I was and what I was capable of. He said that I did a great job and that they wanted me back next year. God was in control. I was free that day. Free to decide what *I* wanted the future to look like. Free to fly.

Tampa Bay went on to sign Tom Brady, Rob Gronkowski, Leonard Fournette, and a host of other future NFL Hall of Famers. I was no longer needed, but I was happy. They would go on to win the Super Bowl that year. I rooted for my friends and former teammates and celebrated their success. But I didn't miss it. I began my speaking career full time and got into broadcasting with ESPN. And soon thereafter, I was on a stage of my own at the Super Bowl, speaking on behalf of International Justice Mission. I was part of a new team, flanked by a new family, living a new purpose. I was now leading athletes from all sports in a fight against injustice.

My new opportunities with Athletes for Justice, International Justice Mission, and ESPN were all born out of that struggle. The tears I shed during those

I said earlier that this is not so much a "how to" book as a "let's do" book. But ultimately, every changemaker has to take that journey from dream to reality.

two months in West Seneca were the water my dreams needed to grow. Saying no to the NFL allowed me to say yes to my future. Sometimes saying no opens doors.

MY STORY AND YOUR STORY

I said earlier that this is not so much a "how to" book as a "let's do" book. I meant that. There's been some practical advice in here—steps you can take to unlock your potential to dream big, count the cost, and become a changemaker. But ultimately, every changemaker has to take that journey from dream to reality.

For me, the true stories of changemakers who came before me were instrumental in that process. My dad's stories filled my imagination and set my heart on fire for serving other people. Listening to Azariah and other kids in the neighborhood gave birth to the Austin Harvest food mart. My passion for the work I do with IJM started with listening to abuse survivors. The list goes on.

Your big change may hinge on hearing my little story. And the change I need to make may hinge on me hearing yours. Your story is unique. No one else has what you have. No one else has experienced what you've experienced *how* you've experienced it. No one.

I'm a middle kid. Though my brother and I both played football at the same school, we have vastly different experiences. Though we both played in the NFL, we have vastly different stories. Though we came from the same womb with the same parents, we have vastly different personalities.

Sharing your story may be the key to unlocking someone's potential, giving them the courage to take that first step. So when you see me on set or in the city, share your story with me. I'd love to hear it.

The reason many of us refrain from making the changes we want to see in this world is that we're afraid. We're afraid of failure, of falling, of looking dumb. Maybe we're even afraid of succeeding, knowing that success will bring new challenges. We're afraid that we won't be able to handle the pressure. I'm here to tell you that you are enough. If I were with you right now I'd give you a hug. I'd remind you that you've got nothing to prove and no one to impress. But you do have a God-given fire to follow. What if the biggest change this world needs is for you to see yourself the way God sees you? As a son or a daughter. As a king or a queen. As his child, his best work.

God sees you. He knows you. He knows your heart and is opening doors that you couldn't open yourself. He knows you're going to stumble; he knows you're

Sharing your story may
be the key to unlocking
someone's potential,
giving them the courage
to take that first step.

going to fall. But he also knows that you're going to get back up, because he's right there with you to give you strength and courage.

Follow the fire, my friend. Together we can change the world.

ACKNOWLEDGMENTS

I can't end this book without saying thank you. Thank you, Jesus, for showing me who you are. Thank you for loving me, for forgiving me, for being kind to me. Thank you for accepting me despite my mess. Thank you for giving me friends.

I also need to thank Lukas. We don't get to pick our family, but we get to pick our friends. Lukas has been the friend I needed exactly when I needed him. He's been honest when I needed some hard truth, and he's been patient when I needed some time. If you don't have a friend like Lukas, pray for one. God will provide.

I also need to thank my family. You all have sacrificed so much to let me write this book. I'll never forget your excitement when I told you it was due. "Daddy's almost done with his book! Yay, we get to play with you!!" I'm excited to play too. Baby, Sophia, Caleb, Kelechi, thank y'all for loving me so well.

Ngozi, you are a gift. Thank you for pushing me past where I thought I could go. Thank you for sacrificing your time and comfort to help me follow my dream. Thank you for dreaming with me. Thank you for being with me. You feel like home.

Daniel, I know we just met, but thank you for believing in this book. We could have gone many different directions, but you believed in the vision. You believed in me. Thank you for your belief. I couldn't be more grateful.

To my mom, dad, sisters, and brother, I love you all. We've been through a lot this year, but I'm glad we're all together. Let's keep it that way. Keep on making memories, keep on dreaming dreams. I'm glad we're growing together.

A special shout-out goes to Dayana from ESPN. When we first talked on the phone about the mentoring circles, I didn't know what to expect. Your heart, your drive, and your ability to build are an inspiration. You used your gifts and created an army of people who are encouraged and motivated to be their best selves. To change their situations. You give me hope. You are living out what this book is all about. Change starts with you, and you, Dayana, prove that it is true. The music video was fire. Let's keep on dreaming together.

To all the great people and organizations that I

support and who support me, thank you. Thank you for buying in, for hoping to make a change. Thank you for following the fire. You are the changemakers that I've been waiting for. I love you all.

To the friends I haven't met yet, I can't wait until we connect. Let's do something special. Let's encourage each other, love each other well, and live like there's no tomorrow. No more fear, no more lies—change is waiting.

NOTES

Introduction
1. 1 Corinthians 13:4–8 NIV.

Chapter 2: The Power of Perspective
1. Matthew 5:13 ESV.
2. Matthew 5:14–16 NKJV.
3. Matthew 20:30 NIV.
4. Matthew 20:32–33 NIV.

Chapter 3: Dreams Are Contagious
1. Nehemiah 1:4.
2. *Circle Keepers Manual* (ROCA, Inc., 2004), PDF, 2, https://bit.ly/2BlCve7. Hosted by National Association of Community and Restorative Justice (NACRJ), accessed September 21, 2022, https://nacrj.org/.
3. "Peace Making Circles," Restorative Justice, accessed September 22, 2022, https://www.rjssi.org/peace-making -circles.
4. Matthew 6:10 KJV.
5. Nehemiah 6:15.

Chapter 5: Your Dream Is Not Just for You

1. "Meaning, Origin, and History of the Name Azariah," Behind the Name, accessed September 22, 2022, https://www.behindthename.com/name/azariah.
2. Nehemiah 3:23.
3. Nehemiah 2:17–18.
4. Nehemiah 4:1.
5. Daniel 3:1–6.
6. Daniel 3:15.
7. Daniel 3:24–25.
8. "Our Work," International Justice Mission, accessed September 21, 2022, https://www.ijm.org/our-work.

Chapter 6: Be Curious. Stay Open.

1. Dan Wheeler, James Wheaton, and Tasneem A. Chowdhury, *The Historic Chicago Greystone: A User's Guide to Renovating and Maintaining Your Home* (Chicago: City Design Center in the College of Architecture and the Arts at the University of Illinois at Chicago, 2007), 3, https://issuu.com/nhsgreystoneandvintage/docs/final_book_layout_w_cover.
2. Luke 10:25, 27.
3. Luke 10:29.
4. Luke 10:30–35 HCSB.

Chapter 7: Change Only Happens Through Focus

1. Luke 10:40 HCSB.
2. Curtis Bunn, "Black Americans 'Used to Injustice' React to Chauvin's Verdict with Mixed Emotions," NBC News, April 23, 2021, https://www.nbcnews.com/news/nbcblk/black-americans-used-injustice-react-chauvin-s-verdict-mixed-emotions-n1265130.
3. "What Are We Going to Do?," The Gathering Spot,

streaming video, 2:14, accessed September 21, 2022, https://thegatheringspot.club/what-are-we-going-to-do/.
4. 1 John 1:9.
5. Luke 23:34 NLT.

Chapter 8: Dream It. Plan It. Do It.

1. Proverbs 29:18.
2. Habakkuk 2:2 ESV.
3. Mark 9:21–23, emphasis added.
4. Mark 9:24.
5. Proverbs 24:33–34 ESV.

Chapter 10: Follow the Fire—But Don't Burn Out

1. Genesis 2:2–3; see Exodus 20:11 and Leviticus 25:1–12.

ABOUT THE AUTHOR

Sam Acho is a nine-year NFL veteran, writer, public speaker, and humanitarian. In addition to his work as an ESPN sports analyst, Sam speaks widely at colleges, events, conferences, and churches. He is the founder and president of Athletes for Justice and the director of human capital, innovation, and impact at AWM Capital. Sam served as vice president of the NFL Players Association for four years and as a player representative for an additional six. He is a graduate of the University of Texas and the Thunderbird School of Global Management. Learn more at samacho.com.